Praise for Zen (

"As the prospect of living longer than any previous generation is re-shaping our collective view of retirement, the need for financial planning has never been more urgent. *Zen and the Art of Wealth* offers a profoundly new and inspiring approach to connecting financial security with intrinsic happiness. The most important personal finance book since *The Wealthy Barber*."

— Tom Deans, Ph.D., author of *Every Family's Business*
and *Willing Wisdom*

"*Zen and the Art of Wealth* is a book about how to live with a foot in two worlds: the world of everyday financial practicalities, and the world of expanded awareness of and inquiry into who and what we really are. The conversation between Warren MacKenzie's characters guides us in facing life's inevitable challenges with the freedom that comes from being fully present and awake to ourselves, our lives, and our world. If you want to be happy, if you want to alleviate suffering in your own life and the world, this book is a wonderful guide."

— Oriah Mountain Dreamer, author of *The Invitation*

"Just another book written by a financial professional? Absolutely not! While there is plenty of sage financial advice, the in-depth analysis and discussion of Zen philosophy and the inter-relationship between money and happiness make this book a must-read for anyone looking to improve their financial security and level of happiness. Well done Warren!"

— David Trahair, financial trainer, national bestselling author

"Warren MacKenzie is one of the most knowledgeable and principled financial advisors I have met. The insights in his new book should benefit every investor."

— Gordon Pape, author of *Retirement's Harsh New Realities*

"A person's happiness can be broad, or deep, or both, or neither. Broadness measures how multifaceted a form of happiness is. Financial success often creates quite broad happiness: it delivers a vast array of desirable objects, situations, relationships, and experiences. But does financial success deliver the broadest happiness possible? To investigate that, we have to look deep. Depth measures how "non-obvious" a form of happiness is. It's obvious to anyone that getting the situations and sensations they want will (often) bring them happiness. But it's not at all obvious that there's a way to be happy independent of situations and sensations. And it's even less obvious that in its fully mature form, achieving happiness independent of situations and sensations empowers a person to more effectively take control of situations and sensations. Optimal happiness is both deep and broad. Warren's book will point you in the right direction."

—Shinzen Young, author of *The Science of Enlightenment*

"Oh no, not another *Wealthy Barber* financial 'story' was my first impression of Warren MacKenzie's *Zen and the Art of Wealth*. But he breaks new ground in the genre by being the first to address both God and Mammon. Where else will you find a Zen primer that also talks about robo-advisers and a fiduciary duty of care?"

—Jonathan Chevreau, founder of the Financial Independence Hub and co-author of *Victory Lap Retirement*

"Warren MacKenzie makes keen observations on the true meaning of wealth through his colourful tale of a struggling entrepreneur who joins his friend and mentor on a weekend retreat. The entrepreneur comes to realize that while money management and financial planning are important, wealth is ultimately a state of mind."

—Rudy Luukko, editor, Investment and Personal Finance, Morningstar Canada

"Warren has written an easy-reading book that makes personal finance very approachable and very personal, in an almost spiritual way—think *The Wealthy Barber* goes to the next stage. I'd highly recommend it for regular investors and people that find finances tough to get their heads around."

—Pat Bolland, former host on Business News Network (BNN)

"*Zen and the Art of Wealth* is the story of two friends, Dave and Alex, who share an engaging conversation while building a drystone wall. It blends basic financial concepts with the Zen philosophy of enlightenment, or self-knowledge. This book will inspire readers to tune out all background noise and drill down to a common sense approach to financial planning and investing by understanding their own personal goals and what financial security means for them while building their wealth. DIY investors will appreciate Alex's list of 50 things to consider."

—Marie Engen, finance blogger at boomerandecho.com

"In his new book, *Zen and the Art of Wealth*, Warren MacKenzie presents us with a unique approach to achieving happiness and financial well-being. This is an enjoyable and thought-provoking read that may have the reader questioning their level of self-knowledge. In addition to intriguing us about Zen philosophy as a foundation for a fulfilling life, he offers some practical and valuable investment advice."

—Judith Murchison, marketing strategist, writer, innovator

"In *Zen and the Art of Wealth*, veteran financial planner Warren MacKenzie dishes up homespun wisdom about planning and investing. His character Alex spends the weekend with an old friend, Dave, whose business is failing and has plunged him into despair. But while Dave laments, Alex is digging for something deeper. He's leading Dave in the direction of self-knowledge and of letting go of his troubles through the practice of Zen. The overall effect is calming and informative. Mr. MacKenzie is combining a lifetime of financial planning and investing experience with a possible road to happiness through Zen."

—Dianne Maley, *Globe and Mail* columnist

"For anyone seeking help on managing his or her money, Zen and the *Art of Wealth* is a must-read. This book guides the reader on how to approach wealth management through a conversation that takes place between two old friends and is written very much in plain English. Through his story-telling, Warren teaches us the basics of Zen philosophy and the real purpose of money and wealth. If we all followed his approach, I am convinced we would all be much happier, regardless of the size of our monetary wealth."

—Geneviève Lavallée, CFA, wealth manager
and financial literacy educator

"Most personal finance books place financial issues—discussions of portfolio construction, tax planning, understanding capital markets, and more—in the foreground. *Zen and the Art of Wealth* is a different kind of book, because it locates financial matters in the background while bringing much deeper questions to the surface. Where do our ideas about financial success come from? How can we recover from financial setbacks? Do our ideas about financial success help us or hinder us in being happy and at peace in life? Warm, well-written and engaging, this book has much to offer the reader who is seeking new insights into how to approach all elements of their finances."

—Alexandra Macqueen, CFP, co-author of
*Pensionize Your Nest Egg: How to Use Product
Allocation to Create a Guaranteed Income for Life*

ZEN
AND THE
ART OF
WEALTH

Finding Your Way to Happiness
and Financial Security

Warren MacKenzie

SELF-HELP AND FINANCIAL PUBLISHING

Published and distributed by Self-Help and Financial Publishing Ltd.
23 Glen Muir Drive,
Scarborough, ON
M1M 2C6

ISBN: 978-0-9738022-1-4

Editor: Donna L. Dawson, CPE
Cover design: Colleen Nicholson, dropthefish.com
Page layout: Daniel Crack, Kinetics Design, kdbooks.ca

For my wife, Paulette; my children, Ben, Peter and Claire; my daughters-in-law, Stephanie and Maria; and my amazing grandchildren, Owen, Andrew, Laura, Alexander, Megan, Kathleen, Ann, Peter, Anne-Marie and John. These are the ones who make me truly wealthy.

Contents

Acknowledgments

I am indebted to my parents, who taught me sound Christian values; to Paulette for her patience, generosity, wisdom and best-in-class parenting skills; and to my children, who have given me nothing but happiness. I am also indebted to Yoga and Zen masters, mainly Nisargadatta and Charlotte Joko Beck. My thanks to Tom Deans, who inspired me and suggested that I write this book. I also want to thank Donna Dawson for her advice and excellent editing skills. Thanks also to individuals who read and gave me honest feedback on the manuscript when it was in a very rough state, including Beverley Pierce, Lorna Audet, Robert Steiner, Genevieve Lavallee, Frank Van Luttikhuizen, John Harasym, Graham Byron, David Wells, Irene Fedun, John Bowser, Wayne McDougall, Deborah Schaufele, Shirley Grant, Mark Gagnon, Don Bastian, Don Wilson, Heather Rose, Elizabeth Raymer and Mary Lou Dickinson.

Preface

The aim of this book is to give readers a basic, practical introduction to Zen philosophy and to show that the understanding we can gain from Zen can lead to financial security and greater happiness. Increasing happiness is the common goal for both the individual who aims for greater wealth and the individual who hopes to acquire self-knowledge through the practice of Zen.

There is a common thread in the way one practices Zen and the way one should manage wealth. To achieve self-knowledge, which is the goal in Zen, we examine all the ideas that come to mind and reject as false all those that do not represent our true self. Similarly, to manage wealth or to increase our financial security, we should examine the world of investing and discard any ideas that are based on false assumptions.

In theory, fully enlightened practitioners of Zen can live happy lives with nothing more than the bare necessities of food and shelter. Greater financial wealth would do nothing to increase happiness for these individuals because they know they already have enough.

In reality, few individuals reach this level of enlightenment. So for most of us, obtaining financial security is a sensible step in the pursuit of happiness. While Zen practitioners understand that you don't need a lot of money to be happy, we also know that being free of financial worries makes it easier to have the time and energy to follow a meditation practice that could lead to a greater understanding of oneself. So it makes perfect sense for everyone, including students of Zen, to do what is necessary to become financially secure.

Prologue:

Thursday afternoon

Dave Bradley had been sitting alone, motionless, for forty-five minutes. He had turned his chair around and was staring out the window of his office on the second floor of the manufacturing business he had started twenty-five years ago. The silence had been punctuated by several calls on his desk phone, pings from his computer and vibrations from his cellphone, all of which he had ignored.

He felt panic gradually taking over as he tried again and again to formulate some coherent strategy to deal with the latest blow to his business. But every time he started a line of thought he became overwhelmed with fears, doubts and indecision. His mind raced, making it impossible to focus on a single thought. During almost thirty years in business Dave had never felt so desperate.

Finally, one clear thought emerged. He said aloud, "I need to see Alex—he's a money man." He turned and typed a quick email.

Moments later, Alex Roy's cellphone pinged. He was pleasantly surprised to see an email from his old friend. But his pleasure turned to concern when he read that Dave had terrible news and needed to talk to someone. Could they, Dave asked, meet at Alex's farm on the weekend for a long talk?

Alex replied that he was already at the farm and invited Dave to come down the next morning and he'd have the coffee ready. Hoping to lighten Dave's mood even a little, Alex also told him that no matter what the problem, he believed the best therapy was physical labor and he had plans to get Dave working on the latest ten-foot section of Alex's drystone wall.

Alex's hobby farm was a two-hour drive east of Toronto; Alex and his wife, Marie, spent most weekends there puttering, relaxing and entertaining friends and family. In the summer Alex could often be found working on the drystone wall.

Alex and Marie planned that eventually Alex would retire from his position as a principal with an investment counseling firm and when that happened he and Marie would move from the city and live full-time at the farm. In the city, Marie was very involved with grandchildren and other family so about once every month or so Alex spent a weekend at the farm alone or with friends. One particular group got together twice a year for what they called the "medical retreat," during which they worked on their social interaction skills—and their poker strategies.

Having grown up in the same small town in Nova Scotia, Dave and Alex had been friends for over fifty years. They had a tradition of getting together a couple of times each year for canoeing, camping or simply to reminisce over a few drinks, but Dave had been preoccupied with his work recently and it had been over a year since he'd spent a weekend with Alex.

1

Friday

Friday morning.

What does it mean to be wealthy?

On Friday morning Dave was up early and on the road by 6:30. During the three-hour drive from his home to Alex's farm, Dave thought about how best to explain to his friend his financial problems and the pros and cons of the choice he had to make about his business. He could not imagine how things would ever be okay again. But Alex was an accountant and a financial advisor and he also had some sort of philosophy of life that let him enjoy life regardless of the challenges he faced, so if anyone could help Dave sort it out, it was Alex.

Dave stopped for breakfast at McDonald's and arrived at the farm around 10:00 AM. Though the sun was high in the sky when he arrived, it reached the farm lane through the dense trees only enough to dapple the dirt track and flash on the windshield intermittently. Dave didn't notice.

The farmhouse had been built in 1860 using local stone, and a stone walkway led from the front door to where Dave parked his truck. As he pulled up in front of the house, Alex came out to greet him. The two old friends hugged each other and went directly to the kitchen, where Alex poured two cups of coffee.

"So what's going on?" Alex asked after Dave settled in, holding his coffee mug in both hands.

The two sat at the kitchen table and over the next two hours and a lot more coffee, Dave explained how his surgical instrument manufacturing business was collapsing. His company had been profitable for many years but technology, a new and well-funded competitor and the loss of a major customer had caused cash-flow problems and triggered the bank to call the loan. When that happened, two key members of Dave's team moved to the new competitor, taking three of the company's biggest clients with them. Dave had already laid off employees. He had been keeping the company afloat with sizable injections of his own money. What had been troubling him the most over the past day or so was that he now had to make a decision to either accept an offer of $1 million for his shares or to mortgage the family home to the maximum possible and inject that cash into the company for desperately needed working capital.

Dave described to Alex how it felt to lose everything—his life's work was down the drain. He had gone from having a net worth of over $15 million to having nothing except his home, and the whole thing had happened within six months. Until recently, Dave felt he had been living the dream. He was successful in business, healthy and athletic and married to an intelligent, supportive wife. His children, Sue, Steve and Don, were all doing well and thanks to Steve and his wife, Jane, he had two grandchildren. Dave had a beautiful home and, until recently, a large investment portfolio.

Alex listened attentively but said little as Dave described how he had grown accustomed to feeling wealthy—he loved seeing himself in the role of successful businessman and not worrying or even thinking about money. "Before this happened I had planned to retire early and give the business to Don," he explained as he got up and put his mug in the kitchen sink. "But that's no longer possible, and I have to say that that is one of my biggest disappointments. You may remember that Don started working in the business soon after he finished his MBA.

"I'm finding it very hard to decide—should I sell my shares and get out or should I mortgage the house and raise the money and stay involved? On the one hand I think the company is worth far more than a million and if I mortgage the house and put more of my own money into the company I believe I could stabilize the business and make it profitable again. But if something else does go wrong we'll really be on the street because we would have no money and no house."

Alex joined Dave at the sink, and after looking out the window for a moment said, "Dave, I've been listening. And I must say: this is good news. I'm quite pleased to hear about these business problems!"

Dave lowered his eyebrows and looked at Alex in confusion.

Alex continued, "Because based on your email I thought it was something serious, like you'd been diagnosed with an inoperable brain tumor, which would truly have been devastating. But losing your wealth is not as huge a problem…" Dave opened his mouth to speak but nothing came out. "…and before you go back on Sunday I think you'll feel much more comfortable about making this big decision. Sometimes we need a serious jolt in order to stop and reassess things—and for you this may be just what you needed to recalibrate and look at life in a different and better way. Let's sit outside—it's a beautiful morning."

Dave followed mutely as Alex led the way to the patio. As they sat down, Alex said, "Let me start by asking what you've lost and what you still have. Does Judy still support you?"

"Of course," Dave replied. "She's in a state of shock but she still believes in me. She's good with either choice."

"Are your children still okay?"

"Yes, they're doing well and have been very supportive."

"Are you in good health?"

"Yes; up until the past few months I worked out every day and I can still run three miles in under thirty minutes."

"Do you still have your integrity?"

Dave sat up straight. "Obviously."

Alex kept asking questions: "Do you have a clear conscience? Do you still have good friends? Do you still have the respect of the community? Can you still feel pride in building what was a great business? Do you still live in one of the greatest countries in the world?" Yes, yes and yes again.

Alex rose and walked to the flower bed at the edge of the patio. He bent and pulled a few weeds, then faced Dave. "Okay, let me get this straight. You have good health, a wonderful and supportive family, you live in a magnificent country, you are highly intelligent, you have solid integrity, good friends, the respect of your community and great business experience—it will be easy for you to get high-paying work as a consultant—and you still think you have big problems?"

Dave ran his hands over his face and sighed. "Okay, I see what you mean. But that doesn't really help at this point. We could lose our house! I know I have it better than many people who have never known what it's like to be wealthy. But I used to have it all, so now I'm fully aware of what I've lost and what I'm missing. It's not easy. I have to straighten things out because my family depends on me. And now that they understand that they're not going to be inheriting anything, my children are worried about their own financial futures and they're suddenly all looking for financial and investment advice."

Alex faced his friend. "I know you've suffered a big loss, but this loss may enable you to open your mind to consider some other possibilities. I'm not a psychologist, but you know that I have a philosophy of life that enables me to be happy regardless of circumstances and my day job is providing financial and investment advice, so I think that over this weekend we're going to have a very interesting conversation!"

"Exactly. That's why I'm here."

"Plus, I also have experience with business failure—remember that airline business that some friends and I started?" Alex shook his head and chuckled.

"Yes, I do remember that," Dave said, "and that's another reason I wanted to talk to you. How did you get through losing that business? Was that your philosophy of life?" Dave asked.

"I got through that business failure by recognizing what I had lost and what I still had. I had my family, my health, my integrity, my education, my self-confidence. The only thing I lost was money. Oh—but it wasn't a total loss; I did recover something. You know those little bottles of airline wine? On the last day, before everything shut down, one of the flight attendants cleaned out the kitchen and put two cases of forty-eight tiny bottles of Pinot Noir in the trunk of my car. Since that's all I recovered from my investment I figured each of those little bottles cost me a few thousand dollars!"

"Yes," Dave laughed, "I remember the first time you used that line! You said, 'look, it's a very special evening—to celebrate I'm going to open a $1,000 bottle of wine!'"

"I still remember how at the time it seemed like it was hugely important, but now I've forgotten most of it and I think of it just as part of the excellent life experience I've gained. And Ken, the partner who brought me into the business, is still a good friend."

Dave pointed out, "One difference is that you were in your forties at the time and you had time to recover. I'm past sixty and I don't have enough years to get it all back. And as I said, I really wanted to leave the business to Don."

"Well, as it turns out you're going to have a chance to leave your children something much more valuable than a business."

"Which is…? I don't have that much insurance."

The sun was overhead by this time. Alex stood and said, "Let's head back inside and think about lunch." As they made their way to the kitchen, he said, "You're going to be able to give them an example of how people should face adversity. Look, do you think your kids are going to get through their lives without ever facing hardships, challenges, disappointments, setbacks and adversity?"

"No, I'm sure they'll all have their challenges."

"Well," Alex continued as he looked in the fridge, "when that happens, now they're going to be able to look back and say, 'Remember when Dad lost the business? He picked himself up, he found out what he could learn from the experience and he got on with his life.' In fact, they'll say, 'I think he became a happier person after he hit the reset button.' Your example is going to make them more able to deal with the challenges they will face during their lives.

"Dave, we've known each other for a lifetime, but until now you've always been too busy building your business to stop to smell the roses and you've never had any interest in talking about anything remotely philosophical, about what life really is. But because of what has happened, this weekend I think you may learn a little about how to be happy, and more about investing than you thought possible in a single weekend. Oh yes, and you're also going to learn something about building drystone walls!"

Dave said, "Well, it would be great if you can make that happen."

Alex nodded as he pulled sandwich meat from the fridge. "Let's start with what it means to be wealthy. When the average person talks about how wealthy someone is they measure it by the real estate or the investment assets they own—their net worth—and other things that can be seen and measured. Someone with $10 million in assets and an enormous home is considered to be wealthy. It's a simple fact; most people believe that wealth is measured by money and financial net worth.

"But let's consider whether investments and real estate are

the best measure of wealth. Let me ask you: what's the purpose of wealth? Why do people work hard to increase their wealth?"

"Well," Dave replied, "I think they want to be able to live the lifestyle they want and look after their families and do the things that wealthy people do. They expect that more wealth will increase their happiness. They also like to be in control and have security and to protect themselves against risks. Wealth helps them do that. And of course there's the pride of accomplishment. Being successful and accumulating wealth is the ultimate competition and we all like to win."

"Okay, let's look at one of these things—the idea that people can be happier if they protect themselves from risks. Here are some potential threats to one's life and security: cancer, a heart attack, a stock market collapse, car accidents, the whole electrical grid going down and eventually there's no food in the cities and riots break out. I could go on, but I think you get the point. No amount of money can ensure that you're always safe. And eventually the worst thing happens—even to the super rich: they get old and feeble and sick and then they die."

"My God!" Dave exclaimed. "You're supposed to be cheering me up, not putting me into a state of deep depression!"

Alex laughed as he set the table. "I am going to cheer you up. But I want to do so based on facts and the truth, not some Panglossian impossible dream. I'm going to show you, I hope, how to be happy in spite of what you see as your problems, and when we're done, I think you'll agree that when you're happy your problems disappear."

Alex assembled sandwiches as Dave sat with his elbows on the table. Alex said, "Do you agree that your financial situation would not be a problem if you were happy?"

"I'd still be losing my business. And maybe my house."

"But you just told me that people strive to be wealthy because they believe wealth leads to happiness. So if you were *already* happy, would it matter if you lost your business?"

Dave thought about that. "Okay, I see where you're coming from. I guess I can agree that if I was still happy after losing the business, and if my family was also happy, then losing the business wouldn't matter *as much*."

"That's right. The purpose of the business is to make you happy and if you're happy anyway the business doesn't matter. But the most important point to understand is that happiness mostly comes from within. It's an internally generated thought and it's only slightly tied to external events. Now I grant you, we all need food and shelter and without these things we're not likely to be happy. But in North America it's not a shortage of food or shelter that's the main cause of unhappiness. For us, most unhappiness is caused by how we interpret some external event. And interestingly enough, the same event can be interpreted differently by someone else and for them it could be a source of happiness." Alex paused to let Dave take this in. "Are you still with me?"

Fidgeting with the cutlery, Dave eventually nodded. "Yes, I think so."

Alex continued. "And there's no question that wealthy people can and should be happy and they also have the potential to do great things if they use their wealth wisely. For example, many wealthy people can and do get enormous satisfaction from helping their family members, contributing to charitable causes, starting foundations and helping those in need. And, they might as well use their money for these purposes, because the wealthiest can't spend it all during their lifetime and they don't take anything with them when they die. Someone once asked a wise man about a wealthy friend who had recently passed away, 'How much did he leave behind?' The wise man answered, 'He left it all behind.'"

"Yes," Dave said, "and I think someone else said, the Brink's truck doesn't follow the hearse to the graveyard."

"But some wealthy people are very unhappy," Alex said, "and their wealth only adds to their unhappiness. Imagine a wealthy person who owns a business and has a $50 million investment portfolio. He's in an unhappy marriage, he is estranged from his children, his employees detest him, he has no friends, he is being ridiculed in the press in the city where he lives, and because of the stress, he can't sleep and his health is failing. Now compare this person to someone who has no money but has a happy marriage, has fun with his children, has many close friends, is loved in his community, feels confident and secure, has interests he pursues with passion, has a good self-image and sleeps well and feels happy. Who do you think is wealthier? Who would you rather be?"

"Of course I'd rather be the happy guy. But better yet is to have the great family and friends and also be wealthy."

"Sure. I'm just saying it makes no sense to measure success against only one benchmark—the 'money in the bank' benchmark. There are other ways that give you a better glimpse into the level of the person's real wealth and happiness. Look, according to general perceptions, you've been wealthy—far wealthier than I'll ever be—so I expect you'll agree with the following positives and negatives of being wealthy.

"On the plus side, of course wealthy people can do certain things that average people can't do. You can travel first class, you don't worry about the cost of anything, you can afford to send your children to the best schools and you can hire people to do all the boring things that most of us have to do ourselves. But there are limits to how monetary wealth can increase happiness. For example, you can only consume so much gourmet food and drink without endangering your health. You may not have to work but you have to keep busy or you'll get bored silly, and you have to act in a certain way to get real love and respect from other people. And rich or poor, we all have a limited lifespan."

Alex added pickle spears to the sandwich plate and continued. "And then there are some problems that may come with money—having wealth brings its own challenges and disappointments. I have some wealthy clients who are unhappy and they worry that the wealth is going to have a long-term negative impact on their children."

"Yes," Dave replied, "Judy and I have had long talks about how we should manage our estate and draft our wills so as not to do more harm than good to the kids." His tone hardened. "Sadly that's no longer an issue."

Nodding, Alex continued. "A very poor person might feel envious when he sees someone with a warmer coat, but the envy and jealousy that a wealthy person experiences might be even more intense if he sees someone with a bigger yacht. You do realize that a super-wealthy individual with a 300 foot yacht that has no helicopter pad can be miserable and consumed with envy if he sees someone with a 310 foot yacht that *has* a helicopter pad.

"Over the years I've talked to or worked with many wealthy people. So I speak from experience when I say that wealthy people have just as many worries as poor people, only they worry about different things. They worry about the amount they pay in income tax, they worry about whether or not they're getting the right rate of return on their investments and they worry about managing their money wisely. They fear losing their wealth and sometimes they wonder if people really like them or whether people only pretend to like them because they have money. And they fear that their children will marry someone who is mostly interested in the money. The good thing is, you're now free from these worries!"

Dave let out a soft chuckle. "Okay, but I agree with whoever said I've been rich and I've been poor, and rich is better."

Smiling, Alex continued. "But Dave, it's also true that a person with less wealth can get more pleasure from a given event—for example, a new car or a special dinner—than does a person who does this routinely. If you only get a new car every ten years you get more satisfaction from the new car than someone who gets a new car every year."

"Yeah, I can see that," said Dave. "I still remember my first new car, and I've never enjoyed another car as much as that old Chevy." He sat up. "Look, I hear what you're saying, but you're making it sound like being wealthy is a bad thing. It's not a bad thing. I loved being wealthy."

"That's not what I meant. Being wealthy is not a bad thing if you use your wealth wisely. But it's not hard to come up with a list of people whose lives have been ruined by too much wealth."

"Of course. My God, look at the lives of some famous entertainers. Very sad. But my problem is, this loss is also affecting my family. My kids have grown up with a certain lifestyle. I paid for their education. I always let them know that I intended to help them buy their first homes, and I've done that for Sue and Steve. They're planning on having me pay for their children's education and helping them establish themselves in business or a career." Dave sighed. "I mean, I know they'll survive, but it was part of my dream to leave a legacy that might have a positive impact on future generations of Bradleys."

"Okay, let's eat, and then I'll give you some ideas that can help your children build their own financial security."

Friday afternoon.

Building financial security

As he reached for the last of the sandwiches, Dave said, "Now that the kids realize they're going to be on their own…Steve's already been after me to ask you for investing advice. Since the three of them are all in different economic situations, it's not like I can tell them all the same thing; they all have different questions. I'm also concerned about my parents. If they ever needed financial help I was going to look after them, but that doesn't look like it will be possible now."

Alex stood. "More coffee?" Alex made a fresh pot and when they'd refilled their cups Alex suggested moving to the family room. The room featured large windows that looked out onto the back lawn of the house and the woods not far beyond. Between the lawn and the trees ran the drystone wall.

Alex turned to face Dave before they sat down. "It *will* be okay. I know your kids pretty well, and I realize their situations are all different. Before the weekend is over we'll go over it all and I'll give you some suggestions for each of them, and for your parents. I'll print off copies of some of the articles I've written so you can pass them on to the kids." He took a sip of his coffee while he gauged Dave's receptiveness. "Do you want to start now or would you rather wait until tomorrow?"

"Why wait. But let me grab my stuff from the truck before I forget." Dave went to his truck and returned with a gym bag and a bottle of wine. "I thought that before the weekend is over we might be able to find a use for this. And I wanted to drink it before it gets auctioned off or something."

Dave stood the wine on the coffee table and sat back down. "Let's start with Don. He's probably in the least stable situation financially since he'll likely be out of a job real soon."

"How old is he now—early thirties?"

Dave had to think for a moment. "Yes, he's thirty-four. And he's quite serious about his current girlfriend and it appears they're thinking about getting married. Actually, Judy and I are a bit concerned because they've known each other for less than a year and we don't actually know her that well."

Alex said, "But my parents probably felt the same way when I got married. I was twenty-two and I'd known Marie for only a very short time. Remember that party where we met was near the end of September and we were married on December 6th. We'd set the wedding date before Marie met my parents for the first time. But Marie has never forgotten the welcome she received from my mother when they first met. She was worried about what they might think of her because it was such a short engagement and she was Catholic and we were Protestant. That was a big deal in those days. But when we arrived at my parent's farm Mom was standing on the steps with her arms wide open to give Marie a big hug."

Dave said, "Yeah, I remember you were a bit nervous about that trip home. We were all pretty surprised about that fast engagement, I have to say. Especially Bobby—remember him? He had hoped he might have a chance with Marie!" And with that the two launched into more than an hour of reminiscing before Alex brought them back on track.

"Anyway—forty-plus years later Marie still talks about how important it was to her that my mother had welcomed her like that and how much that made her love my mother. So whether you know this girl well is not necessarily a concern."

"Fair enough."

"But back to the issue of someone in their thirties. From a financial point of view, there are really only two things they need to focus on. And I know that what I'm about to say runs contrary to what most financial experts will say. But I take a very practical view, and it's my belief that at this age young people should be enjoying life, enjoying family and friends. They should be focusing on developing their skills in whatever type of work they've chosen. This is not the time to worry about how much money they're saving. They're not likely to have much money to invest anyway and it doesn't matter. If they develop two sensible money management habits, they'll have lots of money in the future."

Alex pointed out the window. "Look—turkeys." A flock of eight wild turkeys had wandered onto the wide back lawn and were looking for the seeds that Alex threw down from time to time. "To have wealth in the future, the first thing people in their twenties or early thirties need to do is keep working to improve their job skills and get more and better work experience so they can earn a higher and higher salary. As you well know, the amount that one will have at retirement depends on two things: how much you've earned over your lifetime and how much you've spent. So the first money management skill young people need to develop is the ability to earn a good income.

"The second but almost equally important skill is to learn to live within your means. I'm not saying it's easy," Alex continued, "to live within a budget, but as I've lectured my own kids, you'll have ten times more fun if you do live within your means. Spending more than you earn is a short-term fix and it always results in more pain later on. Whenever anyone has an opportunity to spend money, the reason they decide to spend it is that they make a quick mental calculation and decide they'll be happier if they spend this money than if they don't. When they make this decision they're always thinking in terms of immediate pleasure. They're not thinking about the long-term pain associated with debt and living beyond one's means."

Dave's cellphone rang. "Speak of the devil. Let me take this call from Don."

While Dave was on the phone Alex went to the kitchen and found a bag of chocolate chip cookies. He returned to the living room as Dave was wrapping up the call from Don.

Alex said, "Don't get me wrong, I'm not saying young people should live like misers and never spend money. But if you're spending $8 a day on fancy coffees it adds up. And on the big issues, like housing and transportation in particular, it's very important that they live within their budget. Occasionally they can splurge, but as a rule they have to be very conscious of what they spend on clothes, recreation and entertainment, eating out, socializing—all that kind of stuff." Alex pulled a couple of cookies from the bag. "Here's the beauty of the thing. When they really understand the rewards of being financially responsible, and how much more they're going to be able to spend in the future, they'll start to get just as much enjoyment, or maybe even more, from forgoing the purchase of something that's tempting as they might have previously gotten from making such a purchase."

Alex took a bite of cookie. "The reason this works is simply because we always get a good feeling when we take a positive step toward achieving an important goal. If young people have the objective of obtaining financial independence and they know that one of the steps is to forgo purchases they can't really afford, simply by following through on their plan they can get a jolt of happiness that may be greater than the short-term fix would have been, especially because that would have been followed by guilt and remorse.

"There's a great little book that every young person should read called *The Richest Man in Babylon*. I gave it to all my kids years ago and I know it's influenced their spending and saving habits."

"Here's another useful exercise for young people to consider. Let's say they need a car to get to work. The best idea would be to buy a used car but let's assume they decide to lease a new car. They see one they like that's nice and roomy and has some really cool but unnecessary features. The lease cost is $300 per month and with sales tax and insurance the monthly cost will be $500. Their second choice is a smaller vehicle that doesn't have all the bells and whistles but will still meet their transportation needs and the total cost, including tax and insurance, would be $350 per month. $150 monthly savings may not sound like a lot when you say it fast, but if during their working years they always choose the less-fancy option and invest the difference in a sensible manner, by the time they're ready to retire this would give them an additional $350,000, which might be enough to buy a nice cottage or retire five years sooner!"

"Yeah, I can see that over a career $150 per month makes a big difference."

"Life is all about making decisions," Alex said, "and people generally make better decisions when they have better information. Vacations are another prime example. I remember you telling me that Don and his girlfriend went on a Caribbean cruise. Do you know how much it cost them?"

"As I recall, including flights it was about $6,000. They couldn't really afford it but were both feeling stressed from work and really needed the break. Neither of them had ever been on a cruise and they really wanted to treat themselves."

"I'm not saying it was wrong for them to spend $6,000 on a

vacation, but I wonder if they considered the big picture before they made the decision. Let's say they took a 'staycation' and spent $1,000 for the week instead of six grand. If they did that every year and invested what they saved into a well-diversified investment portfolio they would probably earn enough to retire from those jobs they don't like almost three years sooner. Would it be worth it? Only they can tell. But I'd like them to make an informed choice based on knowing that they'd be able to retire, say, thirty months sooner if, over the course of their working years, they took thirty basic vacations versus thirty fancy vacations. Too often people make spending decisions without a full understanding of the alternatives."

"And who knows?" Dave said. "Maybe they would have had just as much or more fun doing something at home or going on a camping trip. I know Iza did get a mild case of food poisoning on the boat!" Dave reached for the cookies. "And I think this advice might release Don from a bit of worry. He has no money and he feels guilty because he thinks he should be saving. That's kind of the conventional wisdom."

"Speaking of wisdom, how much of this investment advice is dictated by your philosophical beliefs?"

"What I've said up to this point has nothing to do with my philosophy of life – which is largely based on Zen philosophy. This is all common sense. To me, 'wealthy' is a state of mind. It's an attitude. If you know you have enough money and you're happy and feel complete and you're enjoying life, then you're wealthy and you're successful."

"Until six months ago," Dave said, "that was me you're talking about. But now I have neither the 'wealthy' state of mind nor the money or success to back it up."

Giving a nod of concession, Alex offered, "Yes, but keep in mind that we almost always measure wealth by comparing ourselves with others. Compared to most people in the world you're still very wealthy. Imagine a farming community in India where one farmer has twice as big a plot as anyone else. In his community he is wealthy, but by Western standards he might seem impoverished.

"Understand that financial security does not come down to an absolute number or dollar amount. Someone like Don can easily change their perception of their situation and, in the space of a few hours, go from being financially troubled to feeling financially secure. This could happen by sitting down and working out a detailed financial plan they know they can follow and that could lead to the achievement of all their goals. A person doesn't have to suddenly become rich to start to enjoy financial peace of mind, they just need to know that they're now starting to do the right thing and are clearly on a path that will eventually lead to financial independence. Once they start to do the right thing they feel good about themselves, they stop worrying because they know they're going to be financially secure in the future and they start to enjoy life now. As some famous person once said, life is a journey, not a destination."

Dave mused, "That is good advice for Don. But unfortunately I don't know if I'll ever feel financially secure again—let alone wealthy."

Alex continued. "There is another way to think about your situation. I want you to describe a typical day, say, a year ago when you had a very high net worth. Moment by moment— what did you do all day?"

"Well, I was up at 5:30, grabbed a small bite to eat and went to the gym for about an hour. Then I went to a restaurant close to my building and ate breakfast and read the paper. Then I went to the office and met with my team to discuss plans for the day. I usually had other meetings during the day, talked on the phone and answered emails until lunchtime. About half the time I had lunch with a supplier or client and after lunch did the same work activities and drove home at about 6:30. Then I had dinner with Judy, I usually did some work on my computer, checked my emails, planned my day, watched the news and went to bed. Next day same thing."

"Okay, that was how your day shaped up in your role as a business owner. Now you're broke and you're going to have to get a job to earn an income to support yourself. What do you imagine your day will be like in your new role as an employee?"

"I guess old habits are hard to break. I'll probably still get up at the same time and hit the gym, and if the bank wants me to act as a manager while the company is in receivership, I'll still eat breakfast at the same place and my day will be pretty much as it was before." Dave continued. "One good change is that I'll no longer have to worry about making the payroll—that will be the bank's problem. And since it's not really my company anymore, I'm out the door at 5:30."

Alex smiled. "So what you're saying is that about ninety percent of your day will be the same, but you'll not have to worry about meeting the payroll."

"Yes, and I won't feel as wealthy or as good about myself."

"Right, so you're saying that now you have a different idea of yourself."

Dave agreed. "I suppose you could say that. But it's really more than an idea—I am truly broke. Just ask my banker."

"I understand that but I'm going to come back to the fact that wealth is an idea in your mind. Remember you just said you don't feel wealthy anymore. This is where an understanding of Zen philosophy is going to help. But first let's talk about what makes for a happy life, because I think we've agreed that the reason people desire wealth is that they have a desire to be happy."

Alex had another cookie and continued. "If we think a happy life is like what's portrayed in TV shows or beer commercials, we'll be disappointed. Periods of peak happiness—winning the race, achieving a goal, attending a child's graduation—are great but don't last long. Most of our lives are spent doing routine things like housework, working, eating, commuting, watching the news and dealing with family issues. A happy life is not just about the peak experiences we really enjoy, but rather our state of mind as we experience the day-to-day routines which collectively make for a 'happy life.'

"Happiness mostly comes when we stop thinking about ourselves and what we want or what seems to be missing from our lives. And we're probably not thinking about ourselves simply because we're focused on something else. We're focused on work, or we're sharing a joke with a friend, or we're sitting down to enjoy a good meal, or we're excited because our favorite ball player just hit a home run. These moments make up a big part of our lives—and we can have equal enjoyment of these moments regardless of whether we're rich or poor."

Dave, shaking his head, said, "Okay, I can see that some things haven't changed. But as far as I'm concerned other things will never be the same—and they're not better, they're a lot worse!"

"I understand that you've suffered a loss, and nothing can change what happened, but I'm still saying you'll be happier if you recognize the many opportunities for happiness when they do occur each day. In fact, if you keep an open mind, by the time you head home on Sunday I'm pretty sure you'll be happier than you were on the way down here."

Alex wanted to make one more point. "We all want to know that we're getting our fair share, or better still, more than our fair share of happiness. And when we do a better job of recognizing and taking advantage of opportunities for happiness when they occur, then we'll know for sure that we're getting our fair share of happiness. Since most of us are basically greedy, just knowing this is in itself a source of happiness. I think that like most people, until now you've been overlooking some opportunities for happiness."

Getting up, Alex said, "Dave, it's almost 5 o'clock. Are you up for cooking that chili you do so well? I went to town first thing this morning and bought you all the ingredients."

"Sure, but we'll need a nice Cabernet to go with it." He picked up the bottle he had brought in from his truck. "This Riesling's not going to do it."

"That can be arranged. And while you're dicing up the onions let me mention a couple of other thoughts."

While Alex was looking for a suitable wine in the pantry, Dave called out, "Hey—do you have any more of those $1,000 bottles?"

"Like any wine would last that long around here!" Alex emerged with a regular-sized bottle.

Dave added diced onions to the two pounds of hamburger browning on the stove. When the onions were soft he added two cans of diced tomatoes. After draining and rinsing two cans of red kidney beans he stirred in his secret ingredient before adding salt, pepper and chili power.

Alex said, "Everyone agrees that you make the best chili. I think it must be that secret ingredient that I picked up for you and just watched you cut up and add to the mix." Dave stopped mid-stir before they both laughed. Dave set the spoon down and joined Alex at the kitchen table before Alex continued. "So a couple of questions. First, would a very wealthy person who has been diagnosed with inoperable brain cancer trade his wealth for good health?"

"I'm sure there's no question about that."

"And are you in good health?"

Dave nodded yes. "Okay, I get your point."

Getting up from the table to pour some wine and inspect

the simmering chili, Alex said, "This smells very tasty. Let's not forget that when two old friends can get together for great chili and a fine bottle of wine, that is about as good as life gets!"

While the chili simmered on the stove they sat at the table and reminisced about the times they'd enjoyed over the years. From time to time Dave got up to stir the chili and Alex poured more wine. After several taste tests and several additions of salt and chili powder, Dave declared the meal ready.

After eating in silence for a few minutes, Dave looked up and commented, "I think this might be the best chili I've ever made!"

"Yes, this is definitely one of the best and I'm glad you made a double recipe because there'll be lots left over for tomorrow."

Once they'd finished and put their dishes in the sink, Alex made more coffee and refilled their mugs. "Let's head outside to look at the section of the wall we're going to work on tomorrow."

Friday evening.

What does it mean to be happy?

Alex and Dave headed to the edge of the lawn, where rocks of various sizes were strewn near the end of the wall. The wall was now 300 feet long, about three feet high and two feet wide at the top. Its origin was at the western limit of the property and it curved gently to avoid clumps of trees as it stretched past the house and then eastward.

Alex had been at the farm for the past two days and during that time had made fifteen wheelbarrow trips to the edge of a five acre field where generations of the farm's previous owners had left the stones they had moved off the field in order to plow and cultivate.

Dave was impressed and a bit intimidated. "Wow—some of these rocks look *heavy*. How did you get them over here? And are we going to have to lift these tomorrow?"

"It wasn't easy but by laying the wheelbarrow on its side I can roll the rock onto the side of the wheelbarrow and then by grabbing the edge of the wheelbarrow that's on the ground, I can use my legs to push and pull the wheelbarrow upright."

Shaking his head, Dave said, "I'm getting a sore back just thinking about lifting these rocks. This is going to be hard work."

Alex smiled. "It's not work at all. It's fun. It would only be work if we were being paid for it. And besides, we don't actually have to lift all these rocks—some of them can be rolled end over end and moved into position that way."

Dave asked with a smile, "What is the purpose of this wall again? To keep out invading hordes of…wild turkeys?"

"Solely to occupy my body and clear my mind, my friend."

"I see. I know you're dying to tell me—how exactly does lifting rocks and building a wall tie in with your philosophy of life?"

Taking a sip of his coffee, Alex said, "I have indeed discovered a link between Zen and happiness and rock walls! And just while we've been out here I've been formulating some thoughts about Steve's financial situation, and about happiness. See how useful this wall is? Let's go back in and see what we can come up with for Steve." They walked back to the house. "He's thirty-seven, thirty-eight? And how old are his boys?"

"Thirty-eight, yes, and the boys are eight and ten."

They topped up their coffee mugs and sat at the kitchen table. Alex said, "Steve's challenges are quite different from Don's but he's also in a phase of his life where expenses are high and it's hard to save money. Is Jane still looking after the boys full-time?"

"Yes, and I know they're finding it hard to make ends meet on one salary."

"Once again, I don't go crazy with the idea that they should be saving a lot of money at a time when their expenses are high and they've still not reached their maximum earning potential. But if they focus on living within their means they'll be saving *something*, and by the time they're in their sixties they'll get the benefit of compound interest and even small amounts of savings will have grown substantially. And of course the other important thing is that by living within their means they'll not have incurred a ton of debt.

"I think the best time to start to learn something about investing is when you're in your late thirties or early forties. You and I both know that we learn the best investing lessons from our investing mistakes. And the best time to make investing mistakes is when you have only a little money to lose and many years to replace it. What's really sad is when someone makes big mistakes and loses almost everything at a time when they don't have many years to replace it."

"Ouch."

"Your situation is different!" Alex reassured him. "Unfortunately, the people who are most vulnerable to this are widows who left all the investing decisions to their husbands."

Alex continued. "When inexperienced investors are starting out wanting to learn about investing one of the biggest challenges is not so much to learn the things they should *do* as much as it is to learn the things they should avoid doing. The investing world contains many bad and complicated ideas and a much smaller number of good, simple ideas. Young people need to understand that there is a huge financial services industry that exists because people have never been taught the simple, sensible rules of wise investing. We didn't learn about it in school, but investing doesn't have to be complicated."

Alex went to the kitchen window to look at the western sky before he went on. "Looks like it should be nice tomorrow. A few of the bad ideas that need to be explained include the belief that anyone can consistently predict whether the stock market will go up or down in the short to medium term. Here's another thing investors should understand. It's hard for a financial advisor to avoid the conflict of interest that exists when they get paid differently depending on which products they recommend. Unfortunately the industry's compensation structure is such that if an advisor always recommended the low-cost solution, he or she wouldn't earn enough money to hold onto their job.

"Like Don, Steve's a 'Millennial,' and like all investors, Millennials should understand that there are things they can control and other things they can't control—and they need to understand which is which. They'll be able to enjoy above-average performance over the long term by focusing on the things they can control or predict, and by being patient and keeping things simple."

Alex finished his coffee and set his cup down. "A mistake that many new investors make is to think the objective is to try to beat the market by doing better than the return of the relevant stock index. It's easy to be a successful investor, but it's devilishly hard for the average individual to consistently buy individual stocks and bonds and do better than a composite index or a portfolio of exchange traded funds that have the same level of risk. Some professional money managers can do better than their benchmark index but they have investment tools and experience and more time for research because these investment managers don't meet with clients. With limited resources, if an average broker or a do-it-yourself investor could consistently earn a higher return than professional managers without taking more risk, well, that person is in the wrong career."

Dave finished his coffee, picked up Alex's empty mug and took them to the sink, where their supper dishes waited. Alex continued. "The list of factors over which investors have no control, and which they cannot consistently predict, includes things like whether the stock market as a whole goes up or down; whether a particular stock goes up or down; inflation and interest rates; the economy and job reports; and black swan events, such as a government defaulting on its debt, war, earthquakes, etc. These things are totally out of your control."

Responding to Dave's hesitation as he prepared to wash the dishes, Alex said, "Soap's under the sink. Yet, based on my years of experience in talking with investors, I believe eighty or ninety percent of the time they spend working on their investment portfolio is wasted trying to predict these things which can't be consistently predicted. Peter Lynch, the legendary money manager, was quoted as saying if you spend thirteen minutes per year analyzing economic and market forecasts you've wasted ten minutes.

"Sensible investing will give investors the best results over the long term—but it's boring. If young people are investing because it's a fun thing they enjoy doing, then it doesn't matter what they do because they're having fun. But for people like Don and Steve, if it's important to get a reasonable rate of return they should at least earn the return of the relevant index and that's easy to do by using exchange traded funds, or ETFS."

Dave commented, "But I've been hearing that investors should be aware of the high fees in mutual funds. Are exchange traded funds different?"

"Yes, ETFS are similar to mutual funds but one of the significant differences is that fees are lower. Here's another point that's not sufficiently discussed: the importance of an Investment Policy Statement. This is very important because it is the *investment process* that is even more important than the *investment products* and the IPS is a written guideline that explains the investment process that's going to be followed. It helps minimize emotional responses and makes it easier for investors to stay on track. And if they're working with an advisor it will enable them to hold the advisor accountable."

Dave said, "These seem like easy and sensible steps."

"There are a few more basic things, such as eliminating individual stock risk by using ETFS or professional investment managers." Alex spoke enthusiastically as he got into the topic. "Another thing is to match investments to the proper time horizon. People shouldn't be taking risks with money they might need next year for education or the down payment on a house.

"I know many Millennials like to do their own investing but others want to delegate the management of an investment portfolio to a financial advisor. When people do this they should verify that the advisor is competent, which you can do by asking to see performance results for an existing client and see how these results compare to the proper benchmarks. This is a way to easily determine if an advisor is adding value. Of course, if they're using a financial advisor they should get the advisor to agree in advance on what the proper benchmarks will be."

They finished the dishes and sat back down. Alex continued. "People like Don and Steve should spend some time clarifying their short- and long-term goals. They should be in a goals-based investment portfolio, which means choosing an asset mix that can reasonably be expected to earn the rate of return necessary to achieve those goals. If they're invested in a portfolio that's based on their goals, and they're taking no more risk than is necessary, short-term fluctuations shouldn't matter and in fact, short-term volatility can be an opportunity to rebalance the portfolio and lock in profits. For example, if the market rises, the equity part of the portfolio will start to represent a larger and larger percentage of the portfolio, and when you rebalance, some of the equities are sold at the higher price and the proceeds are reinvested in the parts of the portfolio which are temporarily out of favor. It's the old 'buy low and sell high' rule. By following a disciplined rebalancing strategy you can achieve long-term goals with minimal volatility and you don't need to try to predict what direction the market is headed.

"Given that most Millennials like to use the Internet for everything and since they're more technologically savvy than we are, I think it makes sense for them to at least check out a robo-advisor service."

"What the heck is a robo-advisor?"

"Robo-advisors are automated online financial management services that use algorithms to pretty much replace human investment advisors. They are becoming the new best way for the average individual to invest. This is particularly true for folks—like Don and Steve—who currently don't have investment portfolios large enough to enable them to obtain the private client services of professional money managers. Robo-advisors offer different asset mixes depending on the investor's desired rate of return and risk tolerance. All the robo-advisor models use low-cost ETFS and portfolios are designed using algorithms, such as modern portfolio theory. The systematic rebalancing strategy removes emotion from the equation and allows investors to take advantage of stock market volatility to lock in profits by automatically selling high and buying low." Alex paused. "You want a little…" He made a small drinking motion.

"Sure. We might as well finish that bottle of wine."

Alex got two fresh glasses and divided what was left of the wine. "Another important thing about robo-advisors is the fact that they operate under the fiduciary standard of care. So the automatic rebalancing has to be designed to benefit the client—not the advisory firm. With robo-advisors everything is done online, they're available 24/7 and while a portfolio manager will communicate by phone or email to confirm that the portfolio is suitable, you don't have to physically meet with anyone.

Dave said, "I think I've got all that. Or most of it. I just hope I can remember it! But you're making investing sound simple and easy. Or am I just not understanding? I'm also a little bit concerned that the kids will just jump in and start to do it themselves and I know they don't have the experience. They have the confidence—just not the experience!"

"Don't worry—if the boys want to do it themselves I have a list of fifty things they should consider. I'll give you the list before you go. And it is simple and easy. Don't get me wrong—professional money managers may do many complicated things—but it's easy for the average individual to follow a simple strategy to manage money wisely."

Dave sipped his wine. "Okay, good. But I think that's all the investing advice I can handle for one evening. Let's check the news and see how my team is doing."

Alex and Dave moved back to the family room. Alex put the news channel on with the sound muted. They sank into the couch. "This is great—it's wonderful to see you, even though I know you're going through a tough time."

Dave nodded. "Yes, it's great to get away and be able to chat. I really appreciate you listening to all my complaints."

"Well, I'm glad you're here. And I like to talk about how I blend my Zen philosophy and my business of giving financial advice." Alex raised his glass. "But these moments could be wasted if, instead of just enjoying ourselves, we were constantly thinking that things will be better at some time in the future. I mean, your financial situation will eventually improve but if you properly understand happiness you're going to be happy in the future regardless of your level of wealth. The thing that will give you more happiness in the future is to learn to recognize opportunities for happiness as they occur each day."

"Maybe I could use a little philosophy because I know I have to change my way of thinking or I'm going to crack up. I really want to know how you look at things. But you're going to have to go very slowly because this mind-bending stuff is all very new to me."

"We can start by thinking a bit more just about what it means to be happy. Earlier today you agreed that if you were still happy after losing the business, it wouldn't be a big deal."

Hesitantly, Dave said, "Yes."

"Well, let's be realistic about what it means to be happy. It doesn't matter how wealthy you are; most of your time is taken up in repetitive daily activities like getting to work, doing your job, preparing meals, checking emails, talking to your spouse or walking the dog. Occasionally there are moments of intense pleasure, such as when you fall in love, when your children take their first steps and so on. But these moments are infrequent, probably making up no more than a fraction of one percent of our good times, so you can't plan to have a happy life just around these events.

"So while in a happy life there will be some intense pleasures, a happy life mostly consists of a general feeling of contentment. In fact it's the absence of negative thoughts and freedom from worry or regret that are the biggest contributors to a happy life. If you have feelings of unfulfilled desire, regret, guilt, or fear of losing what you have, any of these feelings will prevent you from being happy—no matter how wealthy you are."

Dave said, "Yes, I can certainly relate to that because right now I have a ton of regrets and negative thoughts and I'm miserable."

"Being happy and living a happy life doesn't mean you're never sad or angry. It doesn't mean you're always smiling or laughing. A happy person will experience moments of grief and sadness if they lose a loved one, lose their financial security or face some huge disappointment. Happy people may also get emotional and angry but they quickly get over it and get on with their basically happy lives.

"Dave, you've generally been happy, but as you can confirm because of your recent first-hand experience, most people, even those who are generally happy, have problems. Happy people understand that everyone experiences some tragedy and disappointment, but they accept problems as a part of life and they don't let these things keep them from being happy most of the time."

"I guess you're right. Even when I was wealthy I was constantly putting fires out."

"Yes, and Dave, the fact is that life is a struggle for everyone. Everyone has challenges. I know for sure that there are some very wealthy people who would gladly trade their wealth to have three well-adjusted children like you have."

"Yes, thankfully I'm fortunate in that area."

"And for you to be happy again it will help if you have a realistic view of what happiness means. And it will help to understand how problems surface in your mind—and how they get resolved when you see things differently. When I talk about how to have a happy life I'm not telling you how to avoid all future problems. I'm trying to show that people can be happy in spite of the problems that will always be there. Even if we could solve all our current problems we would quickly create new ones. So the real answer is to learn how to be happy regardless.

"As an aside," Alex added, finishing his wine, "and I don't think this is something that worries you, but there are people who feel guilty when they're happy. They have that puritanical view that if you're happy you must be doing something bad. That's just plain nonsense. No intelligent person should believe there is anything wrong with striving for and achieving happiness."

"I've never had time to think along these lines," Dave said with a sigh. "I was so busy building the company I never even had time to think about whether or not I was happy, never mind whether I should feel guilty about it! I guess you can say I've been goal driven and I can now see that while I was driving myself to build the company I didn't have time to question whether or not I was happy."

Alex leaned forward. "Okay, this is an excellent observation and one that ties in with Zen philosophy. We can get into this more later if you want, but for now, remember that point: that you were so busy building the company that you had no time to think about yourself and your desires. At the time, when you were living in the moment and totally focused on solving problems, you were not unhappy. This is actually a key part of Zen."

"It's certainly true," Dave added, "that I've only become unhappy since I've had time to think about what I've lost."

"Well, you were busy working hard to achieve goals you had set. People expect this will always lead to happiness. Unfortunately there's always the temptation to put off enjoying your life until some goal is achieved. And yet the most important goal for most people, even if they've never sat down to define their goals, is simply to be happy. It helps to understand that we can only live in the present moment and we can never retrieve lost moments during which we *could* have been happy."

"True enough," said Dave.

"It's such a natural thing, almost like breathing, that we don't realize how much this desire for happiness permeates everything we do. On the surface it may appear that there are different reasons for doing things. We do things because of habit, custom, to obey the law or to conform to society's norms. But the simpler explanation is that we never take any action unless we think we will be happier by taking that action than by doing something else, or doing nothing.

"We may not like going to a job we hate, but we do it because we believe we would be even less happy with the unemployment that is the alternative. A person might be unhappy with a spouse but they stay married because they imagine the alternative will make them even unhappier."

"Never really thought about it that way, but yes, I think I understand that." Dave said. Looking at the TV, he said, "Oh crap, they lost."

Following Dave's gaze, Alex said, "Boy, did they ever!" Turning back to Dave, he continued. "In extreme cases people give their lives for their country or their loved ones. Here, too, the person who sacrifices their life for their country or a child does so because in those terrible circumstances of having to make a choice between death and saving a child most parents would freely and instinctively give their own lives."

Dave nodding in agreement. "Yes, I've been there. I remember the time I possibly risked my life facing a bunch of thugs who threatened Susie. I'd do it again in a heartbeat."

"Exactly. In these cases we always do what we do to be happy, or at least less unhappy. My point is it's natural to want to be happy and we should try to understand happiness better. We should all explore what creates happiness and what drives it away so that we can enjoy life more fully."

Shifting his position to face Dave directly, Alex said, "Some people have an unrealistic vision of happiness. If someone dreams of a life where they are always healthy and beautiful, they always have friends to help and support them and they never have any problems or financial worries, then I think we can agree this person is living in the world of fantasy. First, no one, but no one, has a life free of problems and disappointments. Secondly, happiness doesn't come from wealth or *any* external source; it's internally generated, a thought created in your mind."

"Ah!" Dave exclaimed. "This is where the Zen thing comes in."

"Not quite. Still basic happiness." Alex smiled. "Unfortunately, unhappy people look at their lot in life and see problems, and they think that if those problems were solved they would be happy. But some problems simply cannot be solved—for example, a serious health problem, the death of a loved one, stock market crashes—you get the picture. What we have to understand is that with the right attitude, you can be happy even in difficult circumstances and in spite of problems. By all means change your circumstances if you can, but don't put off enjoying life until all your circumstances are perfect, because they never will be. So the first step is to recognize that it's your life and no one except you can make you happy. You're responsible for your own happiness. Don't expect your spouse, your children, your employer or the government to make you happy. But we *can* all be happy."

Dave raised his glass before finishing the last swallow. "Glad to hear it."

"One important step is to recognize how overcoming adversity can be one of the best paths to happiness. We should stop complaining about adversity and use it as an opportunity to learn and improve."

"What doesn't kill you makes you stronger, and all that."

"Yes. For most people in Western society, we have situations—but these situations are not really problems until we have a desire to change them. Body image is an example. Physically we may carry a bit of extra weight with no problem. But when we start to focus on our body image and we want to be slim—only then does it become a problem. Physical needs have to be attended to so we remain healthy, but they normally don't become a problem until our ego, our concept of self, gets injected into the equation. Everything that interferes with our happiness is a mental concept or an idea. And just as we can have the idea that some event or situation is a problem, we can have the opposite idea that it is *not* a problem.

"Nietzsche was right about how problems can make you stronger. Problems should be seen not as terrible disasters but rather as learning opportunities. Because it is only through adversity, mistakes and setbacks that we learn anything.

"Regardless of how wealthy we are, problems always exist. When things are going well we have no desire to learn or to seek the truth. We're enjoying the illusion. But I believe you'll eventually look back at these business problems and realize they were what opened your eyes to greater long-lasting happiness."

"I'm counting on it." Dave added. "And with regard to the decision I have to make—I'm leaning to the option to sell my shares and get out because with a million, plus what we could someday get from the sale of our home, we can have a decent retirement. I hate to sell the company for less than it's worth because I believe I could make a lot of money if I commit myself to it. But I'm in my sixties and if things don't work out I wouldn't have time to recover. No matter what I might like to do, when I see myself as a responsible husband I can't risk Judy's financial future."

Alex said, "Well, based on the recent problems you certainly understand the risk. And when you see yourself in that role and with that responsibility, maybe you really don't have any choice but to sell. You don't have to make the decision tonight. Think about it over the weekend. We'll chat about it again before you leave on Sunday. I'm confident that by Sunday afternoon you'll make the right decision." Alex looked at his watch, reached for the remote and clicked the TV off.

Dave yawned. "This has been a good evening. There were even moments when I actually stopped thinking about my problems and the decision I have to make. I guess that's a start. But I'm exhausted and if you want me to drag rocks around tomorrow I have to hit the hay. I'm going to bed with the belief that my problems are going to be solved by Sunday, so I'm planning on a good night's sleep!"

"Okay, but just remember: I didn't say your challenges are going to vanish. I'm just saying that with the right approach, the situation doesn't have to be a problem."

"Got it. Good night." Dave grabbed his bag and headed up the stairs.

2

Saturday

Saturday breakfast.

Two types of happiness

When Dave came downstairs at 7:30 AM the coffee was made, Alex was adding more toast to the platter of toast and bacon keeping warm in the oven and a carton of eggs and a pan stood ready.

"So? How did you sleep?" Alex asked.

"I slept well. But I had a very weird dream about a rock wall that kept falling down and I had to keep rebuilding." Dave poured himself some coffee and sat looked out the window to check the weather. He turned to Alex. "After sleeping on it, I think I've changed my mind. Maybe I should mortgage the house to raise the capital for the business. With additional funding I'm confident I can build the company back up and eventually sell it for what it's really worth. I've been successful businessman all my life and I believe I can do it again."

Alex said, "Okay, it looks like you've got your successful businessman's hat on this morning and in that role I would not be surprised if you decide to mortgage your home and put everything on the line. If you still think this way Monday morning, you'll have made your decision and I'm sure it will work out fine.

"And with regard to your dream about a rock wall that keeps falling down, today I'm going to teach you something about building rock walls that will last for a century—no rebuilding will ever be required."

"Alex, I've known you for fifty years and I've never known you to be as enthusiastic about anything as you are about this rock wall. Explain it to me."

"Scrambled okay?" Alex asked as he turned the heat on under the pan.

"Definitely okay."

As he cracked eggs into a bowl Alex replied, "I don't know if I *can* explain it. I do like the idea that the wall will be there long after I'm gone. I also like being able to focus entirely on placing rocks on the wall and not being conscious of what work is waiting for me on Monday, or what the stock market's doing." He whisked the eggs. "It's as if Alex the financial consultant has disappeared and instead there is just the experience of rock wall building that's going on."

"Okay, *that* sounds like a Zen thing."

"Actually, you're spot on. Experiencing the moment, rather than thinking about yourself doing something, is a fundamental part of Zen practice." Alex gently pushed the eggs around the pan for a few minutes. Dave found a towel and pulled the toast and bacon from the oven and put it on the table. Alex said, "Bring me your plate." He loaded Dave's plate with eggs. After filling his own, he sat down across from Dave and said, "I want to add another thought to what we said about goals last night. We agreed that setting and achieving goals, or seeing progress toward goals, can be a source of happiness. But we should also understand that successfully completing goals doesn't necessarily lead to happiness. If you want more money, setting a financial goal and making a plan to achieve the goal will result in you having more money. Likewise, setting a goal of physical fitness and following a plan to achieve it will give you more fitness. Looking back, however, you may find that you sacrificed too much to achieve your goals for fitness, wealth or career success. There are many rich, fit and successful professionals who are not very happy!

"I want you to think back for a minute to something you said yesterday. You described the satisfaction you've enjoyed by achieving your goal of building your business."

"Yes," Dave agreed. "I remember saying that and to be honest, building that business was one of the most satisfying things I've ever done."

"Yes," Alex said, "but consider this. You also mentioned that you wanted to help Don financially and leave the business to him and you feel bad because that's no longer possible. Now, I know Don is a competitive runner and it gives him great satisfaction to do well in a race. You've also said in the past that you're concerned that he trains too hard and sometimes you feel sorry for him out there training regardless of the weather. Though maybe not so much now that he's serious about this girlfriend?"

"No, she runs too. The pair of them, out there in the rain and sweltering heat. Crazy. How do you keep the eggs this soft?"

"Just turn the heat off when you pour them in and get them out of the pan before you think they're quite ready. Okay, so Don's still knocking himself out. So here's an idea: if you could, would you consider hiring someone to run the race, win the trophy and then just give the trophy to Don?"

Dave's face wrinkled in confusion. "Where's this going? Because if he didn't win the trophy himself he wouldn't want it."

"Exactly. And yet you wanted to give him the business rather than let him enjoy the satisfaction of becoming successful on his own. You've said building that business was your greatest source of pride. So why do you want to give the business to your son and deprive him of the opportunity to take pride in building something himself? How's that different from giving him a trophy he didn't earn?"

Dave folded a piece of bacon into his mouth. "I never thought of it that way. It's just natural, I guess, that as parents we want to do everything we can for our children."

"Sure, but if you want your child to be happy—and you know that a lot of your own happiness results from overcoming obstacles and achieving your goals—you have to be careful about denying your child the same opportunity to be successful based on their own efforts."

"I see your point. I'll have to think about that one."

"There's a book you should read, since with Don in the business, it's really a family business. It's called *Every Family's Business* and I know it's helped a lot of people avoid the heartache and misery often associated with bringing children into the business."

They ate in silence for a while. "While we're on the topic of children and pride in accomplishments," Alex continued, "there's one point I want to make before it slips my mind. Achieving goals can be a source of happiness and the sooner couples sit down and talk about their short-term and long-term goals, the better it will be. If Don's serious about this woman—what's her name?"

"Iza. Izabel," Dave said as he took the last piece of toast.

"Hey—I had my eye on that!" Alex joked.

"I'm the guest," Dave laughed. "You have to let me have it."

"Okay, you win. Anyway, if they're thinking of getting married, here is one thing they need to do. To attain financial security the most difficult but most important first step is to become clear on their longer-term goals. I know that when young people are competent and skilled at more than one thing it's more difficult to decide on goals. But once the goals have been set then it's easy to create a financial plan that will put them on the path to achieving whatever it is they want to achieve.

"We'll get into some specifics about investing later but I wanted to be sure I made that point: be clear on goals and have a financial plan. It really comes down to deciding what will make you happy. Because it should be a given that the number one goal is to be happy."

"Alex, I totally understand about goals. And that was a great breakfast. Give me one more cup of coffee and I'll be able to lift a ton of rocks."

Coming back to the table with the coffee pot, Alex filled their cups and sat down. "I'm counting on it," he said. "But you're not just going to lift rocks. I'm also going to show you about laying a base layer, how to split rocks and the right way to back fill or chink the spaces between the rocks. I know you're going to enjoy this morning's work on the wall and I have a special incentive for you: do a good job and I promise I'll call the next section of the wall the Dave Bradley section. This way at least you'll have something permanent to show for your time on earth!"

"I like that idea. But don't forget: in addition to teaching me how to build a wall I also need some investment tips for Sue and her husband—I know they're sitting on a few million dollars."

"No problem. I've something to say about happiness, specifically the two types of happiness, that will apply very much to Sue and Paul."

Dave picked up their empty plates and put them in the sink. "Okay, I thought I had the happiness thing. But now there are two types?"

Alex smiled and started to explain. "Conditional happiness exists when some event makes you happy. Maybe you're making progress toward a goal, or you got your first job or a promotion. Maybe you received a nice compliment. Whatever. It doesn't matter what happened, there is something external to you that has created a condition, and you make the judgment that this is a good thing. Happiness, or sadness, is a thought and with conditional happiness the 'happy thought' is triggered by an external event—one that you judge to be pleasing."

Dave was pleasantly surprised. "That's actually pretty simple."

Alex continued, "On the other hand, we say we are experiencing unconditional happiness when we're 'living in the moment' and we're *experiencing* life rather than thinking about life, when we're so fully engrossed in what we're doing we have temporarily forgotten who we are or what we want—so we're not judging—we're just experiencing."

"Is this part of the Zen approach?"

"It is. We all experience this state of concentration many times each day but we pay no attention to it because we don't realize it's even going on or that it's the state in which we experience our true self. In this state (and by that I mean a state where we are free of any of the many different ideas of who we are), we're so absorbed in what we're doing that we forget who we are, or where we are, and looking back we don't even recall where the time went. This is unconditional happiness. It doesn't depend on some condition being met or some event happening. In these moments you have no unfulfilled wants because you're not even thinking about yourself and your wants. Your mind is temporarily focused on something else and you have no consciousness of the role (father, husband, business owner, etc.) that you're playing at that moment."

They sipped their coffee while Alex paused for Dave to absorb this. "Dave, for the last twenty-five years you were singularly focused on building your company. During this period you were, for most of every day, a happy guy because you weren't even thinking about yourself and what you wanted. You were doing what you knew had to be done, you were solving the problems that came your way and you were totally focused on the task. You were working fourteen hours a day, and you had no time to even think about what else you could have been doing.

"With unconditional happiness," Alex continued, "you're fully focused on what you're doing. It might be watching your team at a sporting event, cooking, being absorbed in your work or playing with your child, and while you're doing whatever it is you're not thinking, 'here I am doing this.' As a result, during these moments you're not thinking about yourself or anything that you want and therefore you are free from any unfulfilled desires. You're 'in the zone.' And this is very important: you 'become' the experience rather than the person thinking about the experience."

Dave, listening intently, said, "...Okay. This actually sounds a lot like you when you're working on the rock wall."

"Exactly. I'll go even further: when you're in the zone, with no thought of self, this is as close as you can get to your true essence. This is who you really are when you are free from ideas of 'self.'"

"Now we're definitely getting into the Zen zone and possibly over my head."

"Dave, this part is not complicated. With unconditional happiness you're just not thinking about 'yourself' and the role you're playing at that moment, and therefore you have none of the desires associated with that role. So in part it's this absence of desire that allows you to be free and to live in the moment. And at this time you avoid making judgments about whether the situation is pleasing or not pleasing to you because you're not even conscious of yourself and a desire.

"The good news is that almost everyone experiences unconditional happiness for at least a few hours every day. The problem is that we usually don't recognize these moments when they happen or the experience for what it is. Living in the moment, when the idea of 'me doing something' is absent, means that at that time there can be no negative experience or negative thoughts of 'I don't like what is happening to me.'

"The tendency is to think that happiness occurs only when we get something we want. But in fact, a happy life is more about avoiding things that make us unhappy than it is about living in a constant state of joy with more and more good things happening. For sure we'll take the positive events when they occur, but over the longer term, living in the moment, in pure awareness, results in more moments of happiness. Here's an example of how things get worse when we move from living in the moment or experiencing awareness to putting thoughts of the self back into the picture.

"You love to kayak. Imagine you're on a lake as the sun is setting. The lake is calm, the loons are calling and there is a comfortable breeze. You're totally absorbed in the view, the sound of the water lapping gently against the side of your kayak and you're at peace. Thoughts of yourself and your problems have disappeared from your mind and all that's left is the experiencing of this wonderful moment. At that point you *are* the experience and you have unconditional happiness."

"Okay, I'm still with you."

"But then, the next moment you wish someone was there to share the experience. At that moment you no longer *are* the experience but now you're a person with an unfulfilled desire. You're now a person thinking about the experience, thinking about yourself and thinking about the friend you wish was there. Now you're experiencing a tinge of sadness resulting from an unfulfilled desire.

"You, Dave, were also in the zone, experiencing life rather than thinking about life, during the times when you were 100 percent focused on building your business. You weren't thinking about how your life might change when the business was successful. The idea or mental image of yourself was absent from the equation and therefore there was no unfulfilled desire. But in the blink of an eye you can go from that unconditional happiness to a situation where you're reminded of who you are and what you want."

Nodding in agreement, Dave said, "I guess if you see someone laughing at a joke, at that moment you can be sure the person is living in the moment. But on other occasions wouldn't it be pretty hard to tell?"

"Yes, it is," Alex replied. "And here's a very important point: living in the moment—unconditional happiness—is an all or nothing experience. Just as a woman cannot be a little bit pregnant, you cannot be a little bit in the zone. You're either thinking of yourself while you're doing something or you're not. These moments may last for only a few seconds or for many minutes before you again become aware that it's *you* who has the thought or is doing the activity.

"Part of our feeling of happiness or sadness comes from having an unrealistic view of what a normal life is. A lot of this comes from the unrealistic lifestyles we see on TV and in movies. In TV shows we see people who have money, good friends; they're healthy and beautiful, they don't seem to have bills and mortgages or children who cause problems or spouses who disappoint them. By comparison, our lives may be difficult or dull. But no one would watch a two-hour movie in which the actors spent the entire time doing housework, although that would be a more realistic depiction of an average life. But if people watched movies like this they'd be less unhappy with their own lives because by comparison they would see that they're not missing out on some mythical 'real' life."

"True," Dave said. "Even so-called reality TV shows are not like a real person's life." He got up and added his coffee cup to the dishes in the sink. "Finish your coffee. I'll wash these dishes."

Alex continued. "The reality is that life's a struggle. We all have problems and even if by international standards our problems don't seem great, they seem huge to us because there's always a gap between what we have and what we want and what we can imagine. The result is that people go through their lives feeling that life is unfair because they didn't get what they wanted. The good news is that people become happier as soon as they realize the truth of their situation.

"Imagine you're trying to get home from work and the traffic is worse than normal and you're thirty minutes late. You're annoyed and frustrated because you're hungry and things didn't work out as planned. When you get home you see on TV that a bunch of roads are closed and that many people will require several hours to get home and indeed many people will not make it home at all that night. When you realize your situation is much better than what others are experiencing, you become quite happy with your situation even though it took you an extra half hour to get home. With the additional knowledge of how you're doing compared to others, you realize that you're better off. Well, it's the same with happiness: when you truly realize what it's all about and how your life is no worse and possibly even better than others' lives, you can immediately start to be happier with your life."

Dave agreed, "Yes, I can remember times when business was down but I felt happy anyway because I knew that business was even worse for my competitors! I've also heard that the definition of a wealthy person is someone who has more money than his brother-in-law! So I get the idea that a lot of happiness comes from comparing yourself to others."

Alex passed his empty cup to Dave, who washed it and then drained the sink. "Yes, and as we discussed yesterday, life is a struggle and everyone has challenges and even very wealthy people who might seem to have an easier life also face different types of problems and much of their day may be spent dealing with obligations they would prefer not to have to deal with.

"So give up the notion that a happy life is a life where you would only be doing things you want to do. For most people, happiness depends not on whether or not things are going well but rather on how they *see* their lives and their activities compared to others. If, while you're doing boring or unpleasant work, you think that other people are doing exciting things, then you're going to be unhappy. If, on the other hand, you realize that you are having almost as many opportunities for happiness as most people are, then you can be happy."

Dave said, "I hear what you're saying but I think it's more than just how we look at things. I don't think a positive attitude is enough for someone who lives in a dangerous neighborhood, below the poverty line, unemployed or working at a job they hate and they see no way to break free from their situation."

Alex replied, "Well, I'm not trying to solve all the problems of the world and no one has a solution to eradicate poverty. That's why in a compassionate society we need to look after people who need help. But I am saying that for at least a few hours each day most of the people who live below the poverty line do experience the same level of happiness that is enjoyed by the richest one-tenth of one percent of the population. They have an equal level of happiness during those times when they're living in the moment. It may be when they're playing with their child, when they're in the arms of their lover or when they're watching their favorite TV show. And I'm also saying that these hard-working people could enjoy a bit more happiness each day if they understood the source of happiness and if they understood that they are more than the current idea they hold of themselves. So while understanding who they really are may not solve all their problems it will make their lives a little bit more enjoyable."

Alex concluded, "Does that help explain why some basic understanding of how we experience happiness can lead to greater happiness?"

Nodding, Dave said, "Yes, I think so."

"On the other thing you said you wanted to discuss, how about your daughter? Are she and her husband still doing well?"

Dave handed the now-dry frying pan to Alex. "I don't know where this goes." Alex put the pan away. "Yes, from a financial security point of view there's quite a big difference between Sue and her brothers. She's a psychiatrist and Paul is a cardiologist and between them they make close to $700,000 a year. They have no kids and Paul inherited a ton of money from his grandparents to boot. I believe they already have an investment portfolio worth about $3 million. So they don't need any financial support from me to get by. But they want some advice and I think they just want to know that they're managing their money wisely."

"If they're like most professionals they're so busy they don't have time to properly manage their money. They could be paying a small fortune in fees but have no idea whether they're receiving any value for those fees."

Dave protested, "I dunno. They're scary smart. But I think I did hear them mention that they had no idea how much they were paying in fees."

"It has nothing to do with being smart." Alex replied. "The problem is that most people don't receive the information that's necessary to make a judgment as to whether or not their advisor is adding any value. And it's not the amount they pay in fees that counts, it's whether or not they're getting value for the fees they pay. Any fee is too much if no value is being received—but a reasonable fee is justified when value is received. And you measure value received by comparing your actual results to the proper benchmark. Before you leave I'll give you my list of twenty-one ways to reduce investment fees; but, as I said the amount of the fee isn't as important as whether or not you're getting value for it.

"What investors need—especially investors like Sue and her husband, who have a lot to lose or gain—is a quarterly statement that shows their performance results compared with the proper total return and absolute return benchmarks. If wealthy individuals knew how much they were paying to underperform the market, most of them would move to a robo-advisor firm in a heartbeat. At least then they would expect to do as well as the market."

Dave said, "If anyone were listening they'd think you work for a robo-advisor firm!"

"Well, you know I don't, and if anything, I compete with those firms. While I recommend robo-advisors as the best choice for most people, I truly believe that for people who have more than a million to invest, the outsourced chief investment officer is an even better route." Alex headed out to the back porch.

"What is an outsourced chief investment officer?" Dave asked, following him.

Alex lifted the seat of a bench and rummaged inside. "In a nutshell, you hire a firm that has a fiduciary duty to look after your best interests." He found a glove. "This firm will not manage money itself because it wants to avoid the conflict of interest that exists when managers pass judgment on their own performance." He dug some more, found the glove's mate and handed the pair to Dave. "You'll need these. The firm uses their expertise to hire and monitor active professional investment managers on behalf of their clients. They will usually aim to hire the most appropriate manager for each of six to eight different investment mandates so that the portfolio will be well diversified and they will rebalance the investment portfolio when necessary. These firms believe that just as one doctor can't be the best heart surgeon and also the best neurosurgeon and also the best dermatologist, no one money manager can be the best at all different types of investments."

Alex sat on the bench, pulled on his work boots and picked up his own gloves. Dave put his runners on while Alex continued. "Then they provide their clients with a full and transparent performance report that compares actual results with the appropriate benchmark. They monitor the performance of the managers and if the selected managers start to underperform, or change their style, or if key people leave the firm, the outsourced chief investment officer firm will replace the manager."

Dave asked, "So is this what people like Sue and Paul should be doing with their money?"

"Probably." They headed outside before Alex continued. "But the first thing is that they should sit down and consider carefully what their most important goals are. Given that they already have lots of money I expect their goals are more to do with their professional lives, and maybe to contribute more to society, than to accumulate more wealth. Am I correct in assuming they're not going to have children?"

Dave sighed as they headed across the lawn. "Yes, given how involved and passionate they are about their careers, I think that's a fair assumption." The morning was cool and the grass was still wet with dew.

"So it makes perfect sense that they just want to know that they're being prudent with their wealth."

Dave agreed. "Probably. I think if they were confident that they were doing what they should be doing they'd stop worrying. It's the not knowing, and thinking they're missing something, that bothers them."

Alex continued, "Well, managing money wisely doesn't have to be complicated and doesn't have to take much time. But it helps to think of yourself as the CEO of your own money or wealth management business. If you were running a money management business there are certain reports and types of information you'd insist on receiving from your employees. You'd also want the assets of your business to be invested in a way that's consistent with the goals of your business, meaning you'd want to be in a goals-based asset mix. By that I mean the asset mix and investment mandates are selected and designed to earn the rate of return necessary to achieve your most important financial goals, without taking more risk than necessary.

"Something else they should know about is the Investment Policy Statement, which we talked about last night. This is a document that describes the investment process and it should be detailed enough to be able to hold the advisory firm accountable. Before you go I'm going to make up a package for you and I'll include an article I wrote on this subject. If you think of yourself in the role of a CEO it's easier to know what you need to do to manage money wisely.

"I can't overemphasize the importance of comparing results with the proper absolute return and total return benchmarks. If an investor receives a report that compares their results with the agreed upon benchmarks, and if all is well, then there may be nothing more to talk about or think about until the next quarterly meeting. And if the benchmark comparison shows that things are not going well, you'll know there's an issue that needs to be addressed at the next meeting so the proper decision can be made to correct the situation."

"What's the difference between an absolute return benchmark and a total return benchmark?" Dave asked.

"Well, an absolute return benchmark is the rate of return you need to achieve your goals. Imagine that you have a financial plan and it shows that if you earn an average of five percent per annum then you'll never run out of money and you'll be able to do all the things you want to do. In that situation five percent becomes your absolute rate of return benchmark. If this is the case you're not as concerned about what happens in the markets in general—but you want to know if you're on track to achieve your five percent target rate of return.

"With regard to the other—you understand a price index; it measures the change in the price of a stock market index such as the S&P 500. A total return index tracks the change in price plus the value of dividends or interest that you would have earned if you invested in the index."

The pair reached the end of the wall. "Life is full of uncertainties," Alex said. "Gen Xers may worry about their children, about the environment, their relationships, the economy, etc., but if they follow these common-sense guidelines, at least they can stop worrying about their investments because they'll know they're managing their money wisely. But right now, we've got a wall that needs to be ten feet longer!"

Saturday morning.

The only source of unhappiness

As they surveyed the day's project, Alex pointed out that they'd need the winch to move the largest rock into line. This was a rock of about two tons that the early settlers had moved to the line fence, probably by using a stone boat or with a heavy chain and a pair of draft animals. It now sat outside the path of the wall. With two flat sides, this boulder could be part of the wall, but they had to move it four feet closer to the house or alternatively the wall would have to make another bend to incorporate the rock.

Alex and Dave discussed the possibilities and decided that by anchoring a come-along cable to an oak tree thirty feet onto the lawn and wrapping the other end around the rock they'd be able to winch it into position. After a side trip to the barn to get the equipment they needed, they got started. But as they used the winch to put strain on the cable, the cable started to slip from the rock. Repositioning it, Dave gave the signal for Alex to start winching again. The cable slipped again and Dave decided it could never work because, given the position of the tree, the cable was at the wrong angle.

Dave said, "I have an idea," and disappeared around the side of the house. A few minutes later he re-appeared in his truck. He drove across the lawn and parked between the wall and the house, facing the house. He got out, attached the anchor cable to the truck's trailer hitch and started winching the boulder into place. Gradually the giant rock moved into perfect alignment with the rest of the wall, though some eight or ten feet from the end of it.

Alex said, "That was brilliant!"

After spending about an hour placing smaller rocks into position, the wall had moved noticeably closer to the boulder. With a satisfied look, Dave said, "Now I understand why you're having so much fun building this wall. That boulder hadn't been moved for maybe a couple hundred years and I'm pretty sure it will never move again. I think I should carve my name on it!"

"Yes!" Alex smiled. "And Dave, where did your troubles go when you were straining and totally focused on moving that rock, and then on building the wall toward it?"

Dave paused. "I guess they kind of disappeared when I was so focused on something else."

"Exactly. Your troubles disappeared. Because you 'disappeared.' Of course by that I mean the idea of yourself disappeared when you stopped thinking of yourself as Dave the failed businessman for a moment. While we were moving the rock you had no desire for anything except moving the rock. You were not unhappy during that time because you weren't thinking about yourself or the desire to recover your wealth."

Dave began to speak but seemed to lose his thought and halted. Alex continued. "Speaking of desires, do you know the one and only cause of unhappiness?"

"I'm not certain—but I have a feeling you're going to tell me."

Alex laughed. "Okay, you've talked me into it." Sitting on a completed section of the wall, Alex explained. "In Zen we believe that all unhappiness stems from one source—unfulfilled desires. In your case the unfulfilled (and impossible) desire is to go back in time and have things as they were before your business failed and for you to enjoy once again the feeling of wealth and success. So let's look more closely at these unfulfilled desires—the things that rob us of happiness."

Looking thoughtful, Dave replied, "I can see that if a person has the desire for $100 million and that's not happening, that could be a source of unhappiness. But what if the desire is for genuinely good things like world peace or to protect the environment?"

"It doesn't matter whether the desire is to be wealthy or for world peace. If there is something you wish you had and don't have, it will be a source of unhappiness. Most of us have some experience with unfulfilled desires. It could be the desire for wealth or financial security, for health, children doing well or more success and recognition at work. Whatever. What's important to understand is that it's impossible to fulfill all of our desires. We're guaranteed to always have unfulfilled desires because as soon as we get the thing we want, we think of something else we want. Our imagination can always create newer, bigger and better images, whether it's for a new home, even greater success for our children, or more wealth. We can always compare ourselves with others so we can always see something that seems better. Unless you're Bill Gates, you can always compare yourself to someone with greater wealth."

Moving to a more comfortable position on the wall, Alex said, "If we have the best of everything we'll start to want impossible things like never growing old, world peace and a summer that lasts twelve months. If we pay attention to these ever-increasing desires we end up on a treadmill and we can never be happy until we decide to get off. And we get off the treadmill by realizing that it's impossible to fulfill all of our desires and that the most lasting happiness comes not from fulfilling desires but from *eliminating* desires. In Zen, the key to eliminating desire is to understand who it is that has the desire."

Dave protested, "Well, I have two problems with that. First, the 'who' is obvious, it's me. And second, I think having desires is a good thing. If you're always content with what you have you would have no incentive to improve and grow. I wouldn't have built my business if I didn't have a strong desire to succeed."

Alex nodded, "We can come back to the 'who' point later, because that is the core of Zen philosophy. And I agree—there's no question that dissatisfaction and desire can motivate us to achieve great things. But here is the question: do you want advancement in your career and improved financial circumstances, or do you want *happiness*? You have a choice. You can always want more and achieve it (with the accompanying stress), and then when you have reached that goal you can set another goal which you can also achieve (with more stress and time used up), or you can simply be happy with what you have and where you are." Alex paused for Dave to absorb this. "I'm not suggesting a way to build a successful business or solve all the problems in the world; I'm simply saying what I believe is required in order to be happy."

Dave did not look convinced, but Alex continued. "Understanding is the key and with understanding you'll recognize when you're thinking the wrong way and you can stop *desiring* happiness and simply start to *be* happy. One key, which we'll talk about later, is understanding who it is, or another way to say it is to recognize what role you're seeing yourself in when you have the desire for something."

Alex started sorting through the smaller rocks, looking for one the right size to fill a gap. "Some people go through life looking for happiness and they feel sad because they think others have happier lives. The truth is that we all have an equal chance to be happy. Most people ignore opportunities for happiness because they have the wrong idea of what it is; they're simply looking for the wrong thing. When you're aware of the kind of thinking that makes for a happy life, you can take advantage of all the opportunities that come your way.

"Here's an example. Imagine a prospector panning for gold. He believes that gold always comes in shiny round nuggets. He misses many valuable pieces of gold before he realizes that in its natural state it's not always a big round nugget. Some people throw away opportunities for happiness because they don't recognize them as opportunities when they see them. Sadly, many people confuse happiness with getting things, having success, fulfilling dreams. Getting things is not the key. Since we can always imagine more things we want, getting more things will never be enough to make us happy. It sometimes just makes us greedy and gives us the feeling that we're entitled to more."

The two worked in near silence for a while, Alex pointing out which rocks they needed and how they should be placed. By 11:00 AM it was starting to get warm and Dave took his sweatshirt off and threw it onto the finished section of the wall. He asked, "What's the plan for lunch?"

"I got the stuff to make a Caesar salad and of course there's leftover chili."

Smacking his lips Dave said, "Sounds delicious."

"But before we break for lunch let's see if we can get this thing extended to join up with that boulder. It's only about four feet and we can finish soon after noon."

"Okay, let's get back to it."

"So I was talking about unfulfilled desires being the one and only cause of unhappiness. There's a Zen approach to this which I'm going to explain. But before we go there I should mention that there are many practical ways to increase happiness that don't require any understanding of Zen.

"For example, simple, everyday pleasures provide us all with more opportunities for happiness than most of us realize. In the morning, when you're thinking about how much you're enjoying a good cup of coffee, be aware that no one in the world, not even the richest or most famous or most successful person out there, enjoys a good cup of coffee more than you do."

While Dave struggled with a heavy rock, Alex said. "A great cup of coffee, or a perfectly satisfying breakfast, can only give so much pleasure, regardless of who you are. This is important to understand because unfortunately we often think that if we were rich or famous or more successful, or if the major problem facing us at the moment were solved, then *everything* would be better. This is wrong. The simple pleasures don't get any better and we all have an opportunity to enjoy simple pleasures every day. The pleasure of a cold beer with good friends, or seeing your child take his first step, will not be any better if you become a billionaire.

"So next time you're having your morning coffee and doing your crossword puzzle, remember that solving the puzzle is as good as it gets—for anyone. Warren Buffett and Bill Gates get no more pleasure than you do from this small success."

Dave replied, "That's a good point and I'll keep it in mind when I do my daily Sudoku!"

"Here's another simple way everyone can increase their happiness. It's based on the fact that it's human nature to be happier when you get your fair share and to be sad when you believe that everyone else got more than you did. So simply knowing that you're getting your fair share helps increase happiness.

"Sometimes when we see other people, particularly wealthy people, we think they have more of everything—including happiness—than we do. But when you examine it you'll see that's not true. And when you understand that for most of the day the pleasures you enjoy are just as real as the pleasures anyone else enjoys, you can stop being envious of those who seem to have more."

Picking up a flat rock for the top of the wall, Dave remarked,

"Probably some of my employees might have thought I was living a better life, but they might not have realized how many hours I worked every week."

"Right. Here's another way to explain it. Imagine you found a magic lamp. Or picked one up at the magic lamp store. You rubbed it and the genie came out and offered to guarantee that for five hours every day you'll be as happy as the happiest person in the world; no one would be happier than you. Most people would think this was a wonderful gift and they'd begin looking forward to some superior level of happiness.

"But instead of enjoying intense joy they'd soon discover that the joy of the happiest person in the world was pretty much the same as the happiness they had previously experienced—the great cup of coffee, conquering the crossword, getting together with friends."

"Or building a drystone wall."

"Yes. Or that. The difference would be that now these lucky people would recognize their state of happiness, rather than always thinking real happiness is something more than what it actually is. Almost everyone already has this gift, they just don't realize it. They think they're missing out on happiness. It's as if they own priceless art but have it stored in the basement because they don't realize its value.

"Real joy and happiness can be had while doing any number of simple things, from reading a mystery novel to playing a computer game. If you never look back and just live in the moment, losing yourself in a computer game or a novel provides the same level of happiness potential as losing yourself while composing a great novel or a great musical score that will exist after you're gone."

Dave smiled. "I'll have to mention this to Judy, because she thinks I spend far too much time playing games on my computer."

"Which raises the point that what others think isn't important. If we think it through and decide that our favorite form of recreation is watching soap operas, we shouldn't let anyone else make us think that some other form of recreation is better. Unfortunately many people are influenced by what others say and this makes us feel guilty when our pleasures are not exciting or enlightening or educational. But after you understand happiness better you can feel sympathy for those who criticize you because you'll know that in fact they're the ones who don't understand."

Alex motioned for Dave to help him maneuver a heavy stone into alignment before he continued. "When we talk about different activities or different goals we know that pursuing different goals will mean different consequences. But that doesn't mean one goal is better than another. In establishing goals there's no right or wrong, just different results from different goals. Thinking it all the way through and asking more questions of yourself will lead to better goals. With the wise use of wealth you can achieve your goals and be happy but it certainly makes no sense to sacrifice happiness for greater wealth.

"Unfortunately, at the end of their lives some people look back and realize they spent most of their time planning for the future and waiting for things to get better. They were always taking pictures but not enjoying the moment. The lucky and happy ones will look back and think about all the great friendships they've had and the great times they've enjoyed."

Dave sighed. "I think we maybe need to back up a bit. We were talking before about what you called conditional and unconditional happiness. And I get what you said about conditional happiness. It makes sense that you become happy when you get what you want. But I'm not so sure about unconditional happiness. That sort of seems like a void. And I don't get where being happy with ordinary things fits in. It seems that with unconditional happiness you're not aware of any emotion, happy or sad. So how can that make you happy? I don't see how you can say you're happy if you're not even thinking about whether you are or not. Or is this part of the Zen thing?"

Alex replied, "Unconditional happiness is like what Joko Beck calls joy. She was an American Zen master who taught at the Zen Center of San Diego. She explains that while happiness has an opposite there is no opposite to this type of living in the moment, or as she calls it, 'joy.' I think this unconditional happiness provides the greatest opportunities for happiness. You'll agree that when you're having fun laughing with friends or family or enjoying a game and not thinking about your problems, that is a very desirable state of mind. You can have a lot of fun without thinking, 'here I am having fun.' If you're thinking that way, the next minute you'll be thinking 'here I am having fun—too bad it will soon end,' and that thought is going to detract from the experience.

"In fact, everything you do can be done better and with more enjoyment when you forget about yourself and you're totally focused on what you're doing. When you're conscious of yourself or 'watching' yourself perform you're not likely to perform as well as if you're totally focused on the performance. Imagine a professional athlete, say a pitcher for a major league baseball team. When they're at their best, pitching strikes, they're not thinking about themselves or how they appear on TV. They're so engrossed in the game they're aware of nothing else. Or Tiger Woods when he's playing at his best. At that time he's entirely focused on his game. Indeed one of the main differences between the average athlete and the professional is the fact that professional athletes are able to forget their self-image and focus entirely on the game. During these periods they're experiencing pure awareness and in their mind at that moment there is no concept of self or identity."

Dave smiled as he understood. "I remember when we had that pool tournament with your boys. I was shooting my best game ever and then Kevin asked me what I was doing differently and then as I tried to watch myself—my game totally fell apart!"

"Exactly. I remember hearing an interesting quote from Johnny Miller, who led the Masters by two with four holes to play in 1971—only to see Coody win by two shots. Miller said, 'On the fifteenth hole I started thinking how I'd look in the green jacket; the next thing I know, they're giving it to Charley Coody.'"

Alex continued. "So from the point of view of temporarily stopping all thoughts of self, the 'happiness' result is the same whether you're playing the game yourself or you're a spectator entirely focused on watching your team play. We often think that doing something is better than watching others do it, and maybe it is, but from the point of view of being in the zone and not thinking about self it makes no difference."

Alex took a couple of long steps back to admire their progress before he continued. "And you should know that this is another case where you're all in or you're not in at all. It's like an on/off switch—there's nothing in between. You can't be living in the moment a little bit. You've either forgotten about yourself totally or you're thinking about what you're doing and how you're looking and performing." He gestured at the wall. "Pretty good, eh?"

After they both admired the wall for a moment, Alex continued. "Whether you're a professional athlete or a parent spending time with your child, success comes from focusing entirely on the task at hand and forgetting about yourself and what you desire. This is what quality time with children is supposed to mean. No one is better than children at seeing through failed attempts at 'quality time.' With genuine quality time you've forgotten about everything else except your child and you're truly present with them. If you're thinking about work you might as well be at work because both your child and your work are suffering from your divided attention."

Dave became thoughtful before responding. "I'm afraid I'm guilty of mentally trying to solve work problems when I was supposed to be spending time with the family. Judy would often recognize my glazed look and ask me to come back to the here and now. But," he said, defending himself, "I had a lot of problems in the business and ultimately I was the one who had to make the decisions."

Alex agreed. "We all naturally want to solve—or better still avoid—problems. We don't like pain and embarrassment; that's why adversity and mistakes are the teachers that help us learn how to avoid repeating unpleasant experiences. If you stop for a minute and think of the accomplishment that gives you the greatest pride today, was there not a difficulty that you overcame that made the accomplishment noteworthy? If you hadn't faced that difficulty you wouldn't feel the same sense of accomplishment. But at the time, the difficulty may have seemed insurmountable."

"To be realistic, though," Dave said, "I didn't exactly solve all my problems, so I'm not sure if I can really bathe in that sense of accomplishment."

"I think success," Alex interjected, "and a happy life come from trying things, failing and then trying again. You know, they say that on your deathbed you don't regret the things you tried and failed at, you regret the things you didn't do."

Dave conceded with a nod.

Alex continued. "The same applies to almost everything we do. If it were easy to shoot a low-seventies golf game, golf would lose its appeal. If you didn't work so hard you wouldn't get as much satisfaction from your weekends. Some loneliness is necessary before you can really appreciate your spouse or a friend. The more difficult the challenge, the greater the satisfaction you get from successfully completing it. We should practice looking at every difficulty as an opportunity for learning and improvement and greater happiness. When you have a problem or a hardship, instead of cursing your bad luck, make it a habit to reflect for a moment and consider how you will turn it into a longer-term advantage."

Dave nodded. "I do agree with all that.

"We've all had our share of problems," Alex said, "but problems help us understand our strengths and weaknesses. I remember on one occasion I had two key employees leave my company and go to a competitor. Following that I became almost overwhelmed trying to serve my clients. The problem was so severe I considered getting out of the business. But it forced me to look for ways I could change my business model so that I would be able to serve clients and also have time for myself and my family. As a result I formed a partnership with another financial advisor, invested heavily in computer systems and software, changed my method for deciding on asset allocation questions and changed the profile of the individuals I would accept as clients. The result was greater job satisfaction, my clients were happier and I had more time and a higher income. We learn very little when thing are going well!"

Dave wiped his brow with the back of his gloved hand, leaving a gray smear. "It must be lunch time. Lifting these rocks has given me quite an appetite!"

Alex thumped Dave on the back. "We've earned our lunch, that's for sure!"

Saturday lunch.

Knowing yourself through ideas

Once inside, Alex got the salad fixings, leftover chili and two cans of beer from the fridge. Dave opened a beer and drained a good portion of it. He began making salad while Alex put the chili in the microwave and put dishes on the table.

Alex smiled and said, "Only one beer; we've still got a pile of rocks to turn into another five feet of wall."

"I know, I know," Dave said. "You're plotting to get a lot more free labor out of me."

"Not free," Alex countered with a smile. "You're trading it for financial advice and tips that will help you to know who you really are. All part of the new barter economy."

"Fair enough," Dave said as he tossed dressing into the salad. "But on the topic of getting advice, and advisors, one thing Sue mentioned to me was that they had a hell of a time choosing an advisor, so in the end they kind of didn't choose. They just went with someone they knew."

The microwave squawked and Alex took the chili out and stirred it. "Advice on advisors. Very important. Let's pretend Sue's $3 million investment portfolio is yours. You're retired and your financial security and Judy's financial security depends on managing your investments wisely. You're paying an annual fee of, say, one percent, which is $30,000 per year, and over the past five years, after all fees, your annualized average rate of return was three percent. To keep it simple, let's assume your asset mix consists of half stocks and half bonds." Alex heaped chili into his bowl then pushed the dish toward Dave before helping himself to salad.

"You remember," Alex continued, "that there was a lot of volatility in the market and many markets were down during the year. During your annual review meeting your advisor talks about changes that were made during the year to protect your capital and tells you that it's obviously worked because while many investors had lost money during the year, you made an average return of three percent per annum over the past five years. Tell me, Dave, what's your reaction?"

Dave drank some beer while he thought about that. "Well, I guess I'd say I was hoping to make a higher rate of return—but at least I didn't lose anything."

"And what else?"

"I guess I'd tell him to keep up the good work."

"Okay. Now imagine a slightly different scenario, where you sit down with your advisor and in addition to showing you your three percent return, the report also shows that a total return benchmark made up of a few exchange traded funds, still with a fifty/fifty asset mix, averaged five percent per annum. I know you can do the math: two percent more each year for five years on a $3 million portfolio? That's $300,000, even if we ignore compounding. So you quickly see that you paid about $150,000 in fees over the five years and if you had invested in a simple 'no brainer' ETF portfolio you would have made $300,000 more. Now how do you feel and what do you say to your advisor?"

"Ahh, well, now I'd be upset and I'd want some answers."

"Yes. And might you now start looking for a firm that follows a disciplined investment process and uses best-in-class active investment managers or ETFS?"

"Yeah, for sure I'd be making some changes."

"Right. So this is another reason proper benchmark performance reports are so important. If you don't know how you're doing you could be throwing money away for ten years and never know it. One of the reasons investors stick with advisors who may not add value is simply because they don't know what it's costing them. And if you ask them about their advisor they'll say how nice he or she is. Well of course they're nice! No one survives in this industry unless they're intelligent and nice and very personable. But if you just want a new friend there are many ways to get new friends that cost a lot less money!"

"I'll say. That's money you'll never get back," Dave said. He lifted a forkful of chili. "This really is better the next day."

Alex said, "The idea of getting money back brings us back to something I wanted to talk about. Before lunch we talked about how unfulfilled desires are the source of unhappiness. The other half of that is *who* it is that has the desire to be wealthy again."

"That's easy. It's me, Dave. I'm the guy who wants to recover my wealth."

"Okay. Describe yourself for me."

"Describe myself? Uhh, well...I'm sixty-two, I'm six foot and 190 pounds." Alex looked at him, saying nothing, obviously expecting him to continue. "Ah, I'm a Canadian, an engineer, educated at Dalhousie University in Nova Scotia. I'm a husband and father. I am, or was, a successful business owner and now I'm flat broke?" Dave concluded, hoping that was enough.

"That's it? Give me a more complete description."

"Um...at the moment I have a great sense of loss and frustration. Until a few months ago I took great pride in building my business—it was almost who I was. Now that the business and my wealth are gone I feel I've lost a big part of myself."

"Anything else?"

Dave sighed. "Well, I guess if you want to get philosophical, you might also say that the person I am is also a collection of my education, my experience, my memories and the genes I inherited from my parents. Oh—one more thing," he added. "As of today, I'm also an accomplished drystone wall builder." He finished his beer.

Alex nodded, refilling his salad bowl. "Okay. So over the past months you say you've gone from being rich to being poor. But what you really mean is that you no longer own a business and a large investment portfolio. And as a result, when you think of yourself the idea that comes to your mind is different than the idea that came to your mind a few months ago. As you said yourself, a big part of you seems to have disappeared."

"Right."

Alex probed further. "But would you agree that the person who is doing the thinking and who has the regrets about losing wealth is the same person?"

"Yeah, it's still me."

"Okay. Before I go on to who you are, I'm going to go back to basics a bit so we understand the difference between a real thing and an idea of a real thing."

Dave raised an eyebrow.

Alex continued. "Remember this morning, that one narrow flat rock that you didn't know where to place? You thought it was the wrong shape to be useful? Then we decided to use it as a tie or 'through' rock to connect and stabilize the two sides of the wall? That rock is real, and it didn't change while you were holding it, but your perception of it changed when we found a use for it. For the farmer who had to move it out of the field years ago to get it out of the way, the rock was a nuisance. If the farmer had wanted to build a wall he too would have changed his perception of the rock. But the rock itself has not changed."

Dave was dubious about where the discussion was going. "Fine, I think that's pretty obvious."

Alex continued. "We can extend that concept: over the years you've also changed your idea about me and almost everyone you know, including Judy and your kids."

Dave laughed, "Yes, before I got to know you better I used to think you were very smart!"

Alex smiled. "You win some, you lose some. The point is that everything we know or think we know we actually know only as an idea. In fact the only things we do know are ideas." Dave did not look convinced. Alex carried on. "Think of Sherlock Holmes. You know he's only a fictional character but when I mention his name you get an image in your mind of who I'm talking about. If I mention Abraham Lincoln you know who I'm talking about and you have an image of him.

"Think of my son Andrew. After our many camping trips you know him very well and when I mention his name you bring up a mental picture of him. But as his father I have a different image of him. His mother, his wife and his children all see him in different ways."

"Okay, I get that."

Alex asked, "So do you agree that everyone who thinks of him, thinks of him in a different way, and since all the images are different we could maybe say none of them represents the true person?"

Dave thought about that while he picked up his empty dishes and took them to the sink. "Yes, I think I can agree with that."

Alex gathered his dishes as well and brought them to the sink, where Dave was running the water. "When you're acting in different roles," Alex said, "businessman, husband, father, friend, you actually see yourself in each role and you see yourself differently in each. You also have an idea of me and the idea varies depending on whether we're talking about happiness, investment strategies or rock walls. When you see yourself in the role of business owner you have certain responses to issues.

As a parent you play a different role and have a different set of responses. When you think of something you want, you also have an idea of the role you're in when you want it, and you think you are the person in that role."

Dave stopped washing dishes and presented Alex with the raised eyebrow again.

Alex tried to clarify. "For example, you want this financial problem to be solved. When you're thinking along these lines you're thinking of yourself as a once-successful businessman. But when you wanted your daughter to graduate from medical school you saw yourself in the role of proud parent. When you want to avoid financial embarrassment for Judy, you're thinking of yourself in your role as a husband. Today you're thinking of yourself as a friend and as a rock wall builder."

Dave smiled, "And a very good one, I might add."

"Yes, we have uncovered a heretofore unknown and possibly valuable skill. So you agree that the idea you have of Sherlock Holmes doesn't represent reality, and you agree that none of the ideas anyone has of Andrew matches completely with reality, and you agree that the ideas you have of yourself change frequently. So if the ideas you have of Sherlock Homes and of Andrew don't represent reality, why do you think the frequently changing ideas you have of yourself represent reality?"

Dave replied with some exasperation, "I see where you're coming from, but in the case of myself, I have first-hand experience and intimate knowledge: I *know* who I am." Realizing he had sounded harsh, he tried to lighten the conversation. "And I know I'm going to get you a dishwasher for Christmas. Except that I can't afford it."

"I've always found dishwashing to be a great time for conversation! Okay, yes, you do know yourself, but some of the ideas you have of yourself conflict with each other. And if you think about it I think you'll agree that there has to be something more to you than these changing ideas you have of yourself."

"I guess so."

"So do you think it's possible that a very insecure person with a poor self-image could go into a self-help session and based on what they learn there come out an hour later as someone who is confident and has a positive self-image? I think it might be possible with a brilliant therapist—but has the person *really* changed? Or are they now just entertaining a different (more positive) idea of themselves?"

Dave nodded, "Yes, I would say that the real person is unchanged. It's just that they have a different self-image. I also know that there is something about me that is constant. I know I've changed how I look and what I do and even some of my opinions, but there is some part of me that's still the kid who grew up in Nova Scotia."

"Right. Over the years while your body has changed and your mind has changed there is one part of you that has never changed. Our problem is that usually we identify ourselves with our body or one of the quickly changing ideas of ourselves rather than with our true essence, which has never changed."

Dave seemed to be grasping it. "Yes, I think I see what you mean."

"But," Alex continued, "there was a time—when we were first born—when we didn't have this false idea of who we are. In psychology it's widely accepted that during the first few weeks of life a baby has no concept of self. As newborns we only have awareness of sensations such as hunger, wetness, warmth or tiredness. It is only after a few months that infants develop a sense of identity. In the beginning there is no duality, which manifests itself as 'I' am hungry or 'I' am wet. In the practice of Zen we aim to be able to go back to that state of pure awareness, to be free from the false concepts associated with the different roles we play."

Dave looked at Alex and replied, "Okay, I think I can agree that we have lots of different ideas of self and the ideas change all the time. But I don't understand when you say these ideas are not real. If I can't believe my own ideas, what can I believe?"

Alex put the last of the dishes away. "The truth is that you shouldn't believe any of the ideas you have that seem to describe who you are. I know it sounds crazy but the problem is trying to find the 'you' who is trying to understand and distinguish between the various different ideas of yourself that flash through your mind. The person who is doing the searching can't see the answer because the person doing the searching is what is being searched for. Imagine you're outside looking for yourself but you can't see yourself because you're the one who is doing the looking!"

Dave smiled, "What if I have a mirror?"

Alex didn't let up. "Then you will see a reflection—but you're more than a reflection."

Dave raised his eyebrows again. Alex said, "Bear with me. I'll come back to this. I'll try to think of another way to explain it. But the goal of Zen is to overcome the conditioning that has occurred since infancy and to let us know that our real essence is more than the constantly changing ideas we have of ourselves. Most of the problems we have spring up because we're identifying with the idea that we hold of ourselves—at that particular moment in time. Now before you object and say that losing your business is more than an idea, I know it really happened. But what I'm saying is that while the event happened, it doesn't have to be a problem. This is key: an event doesn't have to be a problem unless we make it a problem."

Alex put his gloves back on. "Okay, we've had a very long

break. Let's get back to work and while we're working I'm going to prove to you that you're just a concept—nothing more than a figment of your own imagination!"

Picking up his gloves, Dave said, "This should be very interesting."

Saturday afternoon.

Real things and concepts

As he slowly rolled a large rock into place as part of the wall's base, Dave asked, "Are these rocks getting heavier or did I have too much to eat?"

"If the truth be known, you've been building most of the base and since I'm doing most of the talking I've had the easier job of fitting these smaller rocks onto the nice solid base you've created."

Stepping back to get a better view of the rock he had just heaved into position, Dave said, "Yes, I noticed that. But I'm actually starting to enjoy this. It makes excellent therapy. Maybe when I start my job search I can advertise my services as a stonemason."

Moving closer to where Dave was working, Alex said, "Definitely an 'A' for effort, but I think in this last section you need to replace the middle rock with a larger one because you have three joints in an almost perfect vertical line. Not only does it not look so good but it also makes the wall less stable."

"Hmm. You're right. I'll switch this one for that larger flat one just to the left. Alex, you realize you're working me pretty hard for someone who is unaccustomed to hard physical labour!"

"Yes, but think about the possibilities. Here you are learning a new skill which could turn out to be quite useful if things continue to go downhill and you wind up deciding to start a drystone wall building business!"

"Well, I am enjoying this weekend—but considering my age I don't think drystone wall building is going to be my next career. But faced with poverty I suppose I'll have to consider all my options."

Alex saw his opening and replied, "But poverty is just a concept. I think we've basically agreed that we can only know ourselves through our ideas. And I'm over-simplifying things here, but let's say there are two types of ideas. One is an idea of something real, like this rock, and the other is an idea that's based on a concept, something that's clearly mental, like the idea of what you expect the wall to look like when it's finished."

Dave smiled. "But we both know this wall will never be finished. It'll be big enough to see from space and you'll still be working on it. So is it real, or not real?"

Alex laughed but continued undeterred. "We need concepts to survive in a complex society, but it helps to distinguish the two types—to know when we're talking about ideas of real things and ideas of concepts." He paused to make sure Dave was still with him.

"Imagine a person from a Third-World country arriving in Canada. Although he barely knows English he wants to see a university, so you take him to see McGill University. You show him the libraries, the laboratories, assembly halls, residences, cafeterias, the professors and the students. You show him everything that is real about the university. You ask him what he thinks. He says, 'it's nice, I see the buildings and the students and the professors—but I was hoping to see the university. Where is the university?'

"You would have to explain to him that the 'university' doesn't exist in reality, it's nothing more than a concept, which is a general idea that ties together all the other parts that *are* real.

You could also explain the 'healthcare system.' In our country we have doctors and nurses, hospitals, ambulances, diagnostic centers, a system for referrals to specialists, drug plans and insurance. When you add all these things together you get more than just the sum of the parts—you get a healthcare system."

Pulling off his gloves and sitting on a flat rock that Dave had just positioned, Alex continued. "We talk about the healthcare system but it too really only exists as an idea, or concept, that helps tie all the parts together. In math, when you add up three numbers you get the total and nothing more. When you add together the elements of the medical community, you get the total plus the *concept* of a healthcare system."

Dave interjected, "Okay I think I get the idea of a concept but I'm not sure what that has to do with me."

"I'm coming to that. And get ready—we're getting close to the big reveal! But let me set the stage because this is very important. Let's agree that for convenience we use concepts all the time. In fact we couldn't function in society without them. We talk about a gallon of gas. The amount of liquid that goes into a gallon was an arbitrary decision made long ago. There's nothing natural about the volume of liquid described as a gallon—but the 'gallon' is a useful concept. Similarly we use concepts to measure distance, but there is nothing in nature that dictates a mile should be as long as it is; it's arbitrary. It's just a concept."

Dave sat on the grass, trying to absorb these ideas. Alex continued. "Think of time. This is another useful concept. It is natural to think of times in the past. We can think of times long ago or times like last week or one hour ago. And we can think of times in the future when things will be different. But looking back we are really just using our mind to remember the past and we do that by activating our brain cells now—*in the present*. And looking to the future we are—*in the present*—using our brain cells to imagine things in the future.

"The only real time is this very moment. All other ideas of time are concepts. If we didn't have watches and a common agreement about time we'd have chaos trying to make appointments. But do you agree that there really only is the present? The past and the future can only be experienced here in the present. There will be a future, but when we experience it we will be in the present."

Dave looked up. "I think I get it."

"Good." Alex picked up a heavy rock. "This rock is real but when I tell you it's going to be the cornerstone that will tidy up the end of the wall, now you see it in a different way. Now you have a *concept* in mind of what the rock is. We've been talking about concepts that are useful, and indeed essential to survive in today's society. But there's another concept that's natural and useful—but also false. And to understand that it's false is the purpose of the study of Zen and I would also say one of the secrets to happiness." He paused to make sure Dave was with him. "Okay, a minute ago we agreed that 'university' is a concept that we add to the real things such as the library, the professors, the curriculum and the students. In the same way, 'Dave' is a concept that we add to the real things which are flesh and bones, mind, memories and experiences. Bottom line: we don't exist as we normally think we do."

Dave tilted his head skeptically. "Are you saying I don't exist? That you don't exist? Did you sneak a few beers while I wasn't looking?"

"I'm not denying that two humans are here working on a rock wall—okay, that two humans are sitting around while they should be working on a wall. I agree it's more difficult to realize that the person you think you are is nothing more than a concept. There is no question that we're here as flesh and bones, but what we don't notice is that when we put it all together we add something else—a separate identity. You have all the physical and mental things like memory and experiences and then you add the overall concept, the healthcare system concept or the university concept or the Dave concept."

"I'm sorry, but I just can't get my head around the idea that you think I'm a concept and not a real person."

"Okay, but when I ask you to think of me you have an image in your mind and you know it's only an image. It's not the real me."

"Yes, I can buy that, but…"

"But if I asked you to describe yourself at this moment you would talk about the current image in your mind and you would believe this is the real you. Even though if I had asked the same question six months ago, when you felt on top of the world, the image and your answer would have been very different."

"Okay, I kind of see your point and I can agree that the idea I have of myself has changed but it certainly feels real, just as the old idea would have felt real then. Right now as I'm sitting here talking to you I know I'm real."

"Yes, Dave, I know you're real too, but I'm saying the real you is the part of you that has never changed. And the objective in Zen is to discover this part that has never changed. And I'm also saying that not one of the constantly changing ideas you have of yourself is the real Dave. The Dave that is an idea in your mind right now is not the real Dave. It's not who you truly are."

Dave sighed. "Now I'm really confused. If I'm not Dave, who am I?"

"This is what Zen is all about: finding out who you really are. In Zen, seeing the truth of this is known as seeing through the illusion that we exist as separate individuals. There is a real you that's more than flesh and bones and more than just an idea. And that 'you' has not changed since birth." Alex got up from the wall and offered his hand to pull Dave up from the grass. "Back to work."

As Dave stood, he put a finger to his lips and pointed with the other hand. "Quietly, slowly, look over your shoulder."

Alex turned toward the other end of the rock wall and saw a doe and her fawn intently watching them. After a couple of seconds, the animals turned and trotted into the woods without a sound. Alex and Dave turned back to their task, selecting and stacking rocks.

Smiling, Alex said. "You know one difference between animals and people?"

"Actually I can think of quite a few."

"Okay, but here's one you've probably never thought of before. Animals always live in the moment. That mother deer is not worrying about what will happen to her fawn if something happens to her. In one way animals may be happier than most humans because they just react to the situation they're in, they don't have an inner voice saying 'oh this is so unfair' and they're not worried about the long-term future."

Dave smiled. "You're 100 percent correct: it has never occurred to me that animals don't have a contingency plan that will protect their offspring! Although that reminds me—I'm now a wee bit worried about my grandchildren. If anything happened to Steve I'd hate to see Jane trying to bring up those boys without Steve's income or other financial resources. They need some form of protection and I guess that might mean life insurance, yes?"

"You're right. Insurance is a cornerstone of financial security. But, if we're getting into these areas, there's something else that is important and that is to be sure you have an up-to-date will. Writing a will is something so many people put off, I guess for obvious reasons. Young people in particular postpone creating a will because they feel like they'll live forever. However, I can tell you that I know a number of couples who have lost an unmarried adult child. And the only thing more terrible than losing a child is having a child die without a will, leaving the parents to deal with the problems of sorting out the estate."

"I've certainly got one, but I have no idea about the kids. Doesn't everything just go to the spouse or parents if there's no will?"

"No—that's a common misconception. There are formulas for who gets how much of what and it's not straightforward and it depends where you live. So you've just gotta have one.

"But back to insurance: it's unfortunate but most people want to avoid insurance agents and any discussion about death or disability. But it is a mistake not to address these facts of life. Everyone insures their home against fire but the chances of loss due to fire are much lower than a loss due to an injury, illness or disability.

"You might wonder why a Zen practitioner would be interested in mundane things like insurance policies, but it's because I believe we should enjoy life to the fullest and for many people that means being free of worries about how your loved ones will be looked after if anything happens to you. For many people, knowing that loved ones are protected is a way to free up their mind to meditate and work on their Zen practice."

Dave said, "Well, I'm glad I set up insurance policies when I was young because I sure couldn't afford it now. I'm just going to turn what I have into paid up policies."

Alex motioned for Dave to help him shift a stone for the base. "You'll not be surprised to hear that you and Judy and the kids all have different insurance needs. So we're back to one of the fundamentals: knowing your goals and what's important to you, which means knowing yourself."

Alex continued, "Take Steve, for example. With two young children, if anything happened to him Jane would be hard pressed to be able to maintain their home and the lifestyle the children are used to. So Steve's goal is likely pretty straightforward: he needs cheap term insurance so that if he dies at least Jane will have enough money to be able to maintain their home and lifestyle."

They took turns wedging smaller stones into place. "Now Sue and Paul are in a totally different situation, first because they have no children and second, even if one of them died suddenly, it wouldn't really affect the survivor's ability to maintain their current lifestyle. But that doesn't necessarily mean that life insurance would not help them achieve their long-term goals. They're probably going to be leaving money to different charities and if they would like to be able to leave two or three times as much to their favorite charities, then whole life insurance is the best way to do this. This works because of the income tax savings that result from having tax free compounding of the income earned within an insurance policy."

"Makes sense," Dave agreed. The sun was moving lower in the sky and Dave pulled his hat forward a little to keep the sun out of his eyes. I'll make sure to pass that on to them. But what about disability insurance?"

"Disability insurance is very important and the kids should definitely get quotes so that they at least know what the cost is to have this protection." Alex looked at his watch. "I'm going to make my famous beef stew for supper so we should probably call it a day. It needs time to cook and at this point, it's still only a concept."

"Don't need to tell me twice." Dave coaxed one more rock into a gap in the wall and then pulled off his gloves.

Saturday dinner.

Why Zen is so hard to understand

Dave and Alex scrubbed the afternoon's dust from their hands and Alex began gathering the makings for stew. As he started cutting stewing beef into small pieces, he suggested that Dave choose a wine to go with the stew.

Alex had only recently started cooking and it was a new undertaking that he enjoyed immensely. He had mastered four dishes and the beef stew was his favorite. While he browned the meat, he chopped onions, potatoes, carrots, one sweet potato and a good-sized parsnip.

Dave returned from the pantry with a bottle of Merlot. "I usually put turnips in. But parsnip—I like that idea. Good flavor." As Dave opened the bottle, Alex pointed at a cupboard, from which Dave then extracted wine glasses and filled them. He got the rest of the dishes they'd need for dinner.

Alex added the vegetables to the pot, along with beef broth and seasonings. He put the lid on and the two took their wine to the family room.

Dave lowered himself onto the couch with a sigh. "I'm beat! This physical labor is quite something! But now I have a question: earlier, you were saying that you and I don't exist. So if I don't exist, where did the 'I' with the sore back come from?"

Both men laughed and then Dave said, "Before you answer that, let me tell you that after today's discussion I've changed my mind and I'm now thinking that on Monday I should take the offer and sell the business. Dave may be a concept, but for many years that concept was 'boss' and after being the boss for almost thirty years there is no way I can be comfortable being an employee and letting someone else call the shots."

Alex said, "Well, I agree that when you see yourself in the 'captain of industry' role it would be very hard to take orders from someone about half your age. If that is your decision I'm sure it will work out just fine. You still have almost forty-eight hours before you have to make the decision and I'll be interested to see if you think the same way tomorrow.

"With regard to your question about your sore back, if your question is really 'how did the universe start,' I don't have the answer. For that answer you look to religion. Zen doesn't try to explain where we came from. Zen just helps you see that certain things that we take for granted are really not true and seeing the truth of these things will help you live a happier life."

Alex took a sip of wine. "You remember I said that to survive in society we have to use words and concepts to communicate. I'm not saying that two human beings are not sitting here talking. What I'm saying is that although we need to use concepts when we speak, it's a mistake to think those concepts are real. We can see your body, you have your mind and your memories and your imagination and your hopes for the future—but here is the problem: you then tie this all together by adding the concept of 'Dave.'"

Putting down his glass, Alex said, "Yesterday at suppertime you were totally engrossed in preparing our meal. You were carefully making your secret recipe and while you were doing that you stopped thinking about anything else. You weren't thinking 'here I am making chili.' By not thinking about your-self or being aware of yourself, you could say that it wasn't 'you' making the chili—there was just chili-making happening. For all intents and purposes, 'you' had disappeared.

"We can really only think of one thing at a time and at that time you were thinking about chili, so there was no thought of self and no idea of 'Dave.' If you'd been thinking about yourself instead of giving the chili your full attention, maybe the chili wouldn't have turned out as well. This is what we call living in the moment: experiencing life and being free of thoughts and judgments."

Dave replied, "Yes, I remember that part of the conversation. Okay, so while I was making the chili I also wasn't thinking about my truck. Are you saying my truck ceased to exist while I was cooking? Did the repo man find me?"

Shaking his head, Alex said, "No, that's not what I'm saying. In fact, if anyone was watching you through the window they might say, 'I see Dave's truck here, and there's Dave cooking his famous chili.' Speaking of food, excuse me for a minute while I go give that stew a stir."

When he returned, Alex said, "But remember, other people can't see what's going on in your mind. What I'm saying is that you normally add something to the flesh and blood and skin and bones and this addition is the concept of 'Dave.' But while you were focused on the cooking you were not adding the concept of Dave so Dave (the concept) was absent. I'm going to keep reminding you of the concept of the 'university,' which you understood and agreed with."

Dave nodded. "Okay, but I know that I'm here now. You might say that I've returned and I'm quite certain that I exist because if I didn't my back wouldn't hurt. I can't say that I don't exist because my bones and joints are telling me that I very much exist. It's just crazy to say I don't exist."

Alex said, "Well, René Descartes, the French philosopher, agreed with your point and he famously said, 'I think, therefore

I am.' It was self-evident to him that he could not deny his existence because the person who was doing the denying must therefore exist—or there could be no denying going on. But here's another way to think about it. Let's go back to when you were so focused on cooking that you forgot about your problems, you forgot about the loss of your wealth, you forgot the rock wall and you forgot you even existed. During that brief period you were really alive and you had no worries or concerns because—and bear with me—the 'concept of Dave' that you're worrying about didn't exist."

"Well, I disagree. I think I existed. I just wasn't thinking about myself, just like I wasn't thinking about my truck."

Alex tried another approach. "Okay, but there was music on in the background and remember you heard that old sixties song and it immediately reminded you of a time when you felt very different about yourself? We can go through old photo albums and when you remember how you felt about yourself at the time each picture was taken you realize that the ideas you have of yourself are constantly changing."

Taking another sip of wine, Alex asked, "Isn't it more reasonable to say that the real you is the life force or the consciousness that creates these ideas?"

"Life force. Oh boy." With a questioning look Dave asked, "Are you saying that the *real* me is something like an energy force?"

"Yes, that's one way of looking at it. The American Zen master I think I mentioned, Joko Beck, describes it as an ever-changing energy field. And you should also know that the energy force or life force or consciousness that activates your body is exactly the same as the force that activates *my* body. In our true essence you and I and everyone on the planet share the same life force. And in that respect there is no difference between people wherever they are and regardless of what they look like or believe."

Dave raised his eyebrows and took a large swallow of wine.

Alex continued. "Imagine it this way. Imagine that the life force is like electricity. So the life force or consciousness is the same in everyone and this could be compared to an electrical grid that lights up a city. And while it appears to be different as it lights up different light fixtures and different-colored lights, it is really the same force manifested in different ways. We know that light bulbs and appliances come in all different shapes, different wattage etc., but the key thing which is common is the electricity that makes them work. Just as electricity is common to all appliances and light fixtures, so is consciousness common to all living creatures.

"Or imagine if a computer could truly think. If it could it might think that it exists as a separate entity. But we all know that the computer system works through the use of hardware, software, memory—and electricity. But if this 'thinking' computer also started to believe it had a life and a purpose and responsibility beyond the hardware, software, memory and electricity, then it might give itself a name, say, 'Dave...'"

"Or perhaps 'Hal.'"

"...and then it would start to worry about 'Dave.' In this case it would be under the same illusion as humans have when they believe they exist as something more than flesh and bones and memory and life force."

Smiling, Dave interjected, "Don't you know that by 2025 most homes are going to have a robot running around the house? On the topic of housework, I'll go stir." Dave made his way to the kitchen.

When Dave returned, Alex continued. "If we talk about computers having desires it's clearly science fiction. Or we hope it is! We know without a doubt that the essence of the computer operating system is software and a power source that is electricity. If the computer is programmed to take action to check its systems, we don't use that as evidence of an identity over and above the hardware and software and power source. With ourselves, however, we have the hardware (our physical body), the software (our brain) and the power source (our consciousness), but in addition we give ourselves something else—the concept of self—which is our separate identity over and above all the rest of it. It is the addition of this overriding concept of self that causes the problems."

Dave shook his head in confusion. "Tell me again—why is this a problem?"

"It's a problem because we start to worry about this concept of self, this image we have created and which we identify with and which we start to believe is the person we are. This idea becomes our ego or self-image and we go to great lengths to protect our image and we feel bad if it seems to be threatened in any way. But we can have a greater sense of happiness if we focus on the part of us that is unchanging. You can call it consciousness; I like to call it the life force. The life force is real and unchanging, and while the flesh and blood and skin and bones of our bodies are also real, although they change as we age, what is totally false is the thought that any one of the fleeting ideas we have of ourselves represents who we really are."

Alex let Dave process these thoughts for a moment before he added, "The dilemma is that it's impossible to intellectually see the truth of what I'm saying. Remember, what I'm saying is that the 'you' you think you are is a concept, just like 'university' is a concept. Intellectually this is impossible to see because, as Descartes pointed out, there has to be someone doing the seeing, someone to make the judgment that you don't exist. And of course it appears that the person who is making the judgment is the real you. You could keep going backward forever, always trying to find the 'you' who's doing the thinking and searching. But although it's impossible to come to this conclusion by following a logical approach, it *is* possible to intuitively understand this when we get a flash of insight from the right side of the brain."

Dave mimed the explosion of his own head. Alex continued undeterred. "Zen masters say that there are two ways to come to this realization. One way is through study and meditation; gradually, you will start to see the truth. In terms of teaching Zen, Shinzen Young is one of the most recognized teachers in the US, and he offers the analogy of walking through a light mist. If you do this long enough eventually you'll get soaking wet. What he means is that through meditation and study, if you hear these ideas stated often enough and in many different ways, eventually you grasp the truth. The other way is when you least expect it: you get a flash of insight."

Alex gestured toward the kitchen. "That's starting to smell good, if I do say so myself."

"Hey—something I can understand! Yes, it smells like I'm hungry."

"If this insight happens," Alex said, "it's best if you're prepared for it. Otherwise it could be quite scary. You can imagine that if the person doesn't understand what's happening, a sudden realization that they don't exist—as they have normally thought they existed—could be unnerving. But after years of meditation and reading about Yoga and Zen I knew what to expect. And it was this insight that has helped me enjoy my life to the fullest."

Dave, looking puzzled, asked, "So what was different after you came to this realization?"

Alex explained, "Well, up to that point, like everyone else, I was always concerned about the 'self' and by that I mean whichever version of myself I was thinking of at that moment. But when I saw that this 'self' was just an idea—no more real than Sherlock Homes—I stopped worrying about 'myself' and started enjoying life without worry about the current concept of self that

I was entertaining in my mind. In the Zen literature, obtaining this understanding is described as being 'liberated' from the illusion that the current idea of 'self' is who you really are.

"And it's not just crazy Zen enthusiasts who say this," Alex added with a smile. He picked up his smartphone from the end table and searched for a moment. "Here it is. In 1934 Einstein wrote,

> The true value of a human being is determined primarily by the measure and the sense in which he has attained liberation from the self. A human being is a part of the whole, called by us "Universe"—a part limited in time and space. He experiences himself, his thoughts and feelings as something separated from the rest—a kind of optical delusion of consciousness."

Dave lifted his upturned hands and asked, "Okay, if you can't intellectually understand this—and I do at least understand how the thinker can't think himself out of the equation—what is the best way to get this insight?"

Alex suggested, "Most experts agree that the best way is through years of meditation. I also found one useful exercise, which is when you're thinking about something, simply remind yourself that the image you have of yourself who is doing the thinking is not the real you; instead there's just thinking going on. Every time you have a thought of who you are, keep reminding yourself that this is not the real you."

Dave seemed to accept this so Alex continued. "Keep in mind that we're so programmed to think in concepts that this is not an insight that comes quickly. I was meditating for many years and I read many books on Yoga and Zen before I was able to grasp the truth of who I really am—or more accurately, the truth of who I am not!"

Alex stood and stretched and moved to the big window. "Looks like dinnertime."

Dave said, "Smells like dinnertime. Let's go see if it's ready." They headed into the kitchen and Dave poured more wine while Alex stirred the stew. He pressed a piece of meat against the side of the pot to see if it was tender and then had a taste. He ground some pepper into the pot and turned the heat off. He carried the pot to the table and dug a ladle from a drawer.

Filling his bowl, Dave said, "I'm suddenly starving! Must be all that unaccustomed physical labor. Free physical labor."

"Not free—you're trading it for happy-life advice and investment advice, remember?" He saluted Dave with his wine glass.

"Okay, then—investment advice. I have a question about that and I think I might even have picked up on a link between investing and Zen."

"Good. I want to hear this."

"This is excellent stew, by the way. The parsnip works." Now Dave saluted Alex before he continued. "If I understand you correctly, Zen is pretty simple: just stop believing things that are untrue. And you're saying the same thing for investing: just stop believing things that are untrue. Am I right?"

"Yes. On both counts it might be easier said than done. But you've got it."

"So when you were talking about wise investment management you made it sound so simple. But to be a wise investor, don't you also have to have some understanding of various ratios and yields and upsides and downsides and God knows what else?"

"Your son-in-law is a heart surgeon, right? If I was going in for heart surgery, do I need to understand the finer workings of stents, pacemakers, embolisms or the carotid artery versus the other kind of artery?"

"No," Dave said. "You just need a good surgeon. But if you're saying you just need a good advisor, how can the average person tell if the person they're talking to is a good advisor? Because they pretty much all sound very smart and the average person doesn't have the experience to be able to make an informed judgment."

Alex put his spoon down and took a sip of wine. "That's a good point—but there is a way to determine if an advisor is a good one. There's just a few steps. First, you ask the potential advisor to pick a client who has an investment portfolio similar in size to yours and who has been a client of that advisor for at least three years. Then you ask to see a quarterly performance report, with the name removed of course, and you look to see if the report provides actual performance results compared to the proper benchmarks. If it doesn't, you continue your search for an advisor.

"What I'm talking about is a percentage rate of return and a comparison with either your target rate of return or a composite benchmark return. It's not helpful how financial institutions will insert several irrelevant indices at the bottom of a page and investors will think they're getting a proper benchmark comparison. Recently I talked with one lady who thought her advisor was doing a great job until I pointed out that the index on the bottom of the page was a price-only index but that a proper comparison needed to be against a total return index. She had been underperforming by about three percent per annum for the past ten years!"

"Ouch."

"Ouch indeed. Another step might be to ask to see a client's Investment Policy Statement. I talked about this before— the thing that explains how the investment portfolio will be managed, what investment mandates will be used, what the proper benchmarks are, when the portfolio will be rebalanced, etc., etc. The document should be detailed enough to be able to hold the advisor accountable. It should also be easy to read and understand. If there is no IPS, or it's not clear, or if it doesn't provide enough information for you to understand the investment process, then you keep looking.

Alex continued. "I'm also very suspicious when I see a financial advisor buying individual stocks and bonds. If that advisor is smart enough to pick, say, US equities better than the best US equity specialist, and international stocks better that the best international equity specialist, and corporate bonds better than the best corporate bond specialist, I have to ask myself—why is this guy still working as a financial advisor?"

As he refilled their glasses, Alex said, "But if the advisor provides a proper Investment Policy Statement and a proper performance report, then your search is over. One final point: something that many people do, though it's usually a waste of time, is to ask their friends for referrals. The problem with this approach is that most people like their investment advisor because investment advisors are generally very nice people. But this doesn't mean the advisor is delivering any value. People stay for years with an advisor and because they never receive a performance report which shows performance compared to a benchmark they don't realize they're almost always underperforming.

"Unless you're just looking to make a new friend, you're going to want to be with an advisor because he or she delivers results, not because they're nice. If investors realized how much underperformance costs them, they would demand to see a benchmark comparison. On a million dollar portfolio, if they underperform by only one percent, over twenty years the cost might easily be $250,000. For most people, that's a lot of money."

"I'll say."

They finished their supper and then went back to the family

room with the last of the wine. Dave said, "I have to say, I do feel like I'm learning more about investing."

"Great!"

"But except for brief periods, I can't stop thinking about this massive failure and seeing my life's work, the thing I value most, go down the drain. I'd almost forgotten about that for a while this evening—almost—but the reality of it has just presented itself once again."

"My God," Alex said, "you'd better hope your children never hear you say that! If they do I know they'll be disappointed. They probably believe that you put a lot of value on knowing they're happy and successful. And they're smart enough to know they wouldn't be where they are without your good example. They might be surprised to learn you're valuing the business more than them!"

"Okay, you're right, the kids are more important." Dave agreed with a sigh, "and I know we did a good job with the kids." He looked out the big window into the darkness. "So I guess maybe I'm not a total failure."

"Good, you're starting to see the light. Let's leave it at that for now. Tomorrow we can talk about my Zen approach to investing and managing wealth."

"That should be good."

"It will be." Alex picked up the remote control and turned on the news. "Should we see if the world's still out there?"

3

Sunday

Sunday morning.

Our true essence

On Sunday morning Dave came downstairs to the smell of coffee and blueberry pancakes.

"Good morning, Dave. I was starting to worry about you—it's almost 8:00 AM!"

"I've missed a lot of sleep lately. So I have a bit of catching up to do."

"And you did sleep well last night?"

"As a matter of fact I did. I guess there's nothing like spending a day lifting heavy rocks to help a man get a good night's sleep." Looking out the kitchen window, Dave commented, "It looks like we might get some rain. Did you hear the forecast?"

"No, not yet—but no worries. If it rains we'll stay indoors and drink more coffee."

Dave filled a mug with coffee and after his first sips said, "So...I know I may seem incredibly indecisive but...on the option to sell the business? I think I'm changing my mind again and maybe I will mortgage the house, raise the money and go for broke. If I correctly understand what you've been saying, a failure is not a big deal. I'll always be able to do some kind of work and I'll still have food and shelter. It's just my image of myself as a successful business owner that will be...well, shattered." He perked up and continued. "But if that happens I'll just start to think of myself in the role of a stone wall builder!"

Alex said, "It's true: with success or failure, you'll still have more going for you than most people. If you fail it's really your ego that will have the problem—failure of a business will have no bearing on who you really are. And you still have twenty-four hours before you have to give them your answer."

Dave nodded. "I was thinking about what we talked about yesterday and how the idea I have of myself as a failed businessman might be the wrong idea after all. As you pointed out last night, maybe I should be thinking of myself as a successful father because I know I did a good job with my kids. I was kind of forcing myself to think about the kids last night, and maybe taking a more positive line of thinking might have been part of what helped me sleep a bit better."

Looking up from the griddle, Alex responded, "You'll definitely be happier if you have a positive self-image rather than a negative one. But that's not what Zen is all about. It's not just that the negative thought is wrong. The point I was making is that all of these 'this is who I am' thoughts are wrong." He found a glass jar of syrup in the cupboard and passed it to Dave, who set it on the table. "This comes from our neighbors down the lane. It's hard to believe something this good flows out of a tree."

Alex continued. "In Zen, we're trying to find the truth of who we really are—not by sorting through ideas to see which is real, but by examining ideas and eliminating all those that are clearly false. Over time, when you've recognized and rejected all the false ideas you have of yourself, what's left is the truth and that's the part that represents who you really are. All of your problems stem from believing that one or another of the 'this is who I am' ideas that pop into your head are real. A few minutes ago you looked out the window, you looked at the sky and said 'it looks like rain.' For those few seconds there was no idea of self in your mind. During that moment, while you were looking at the sky and wondering about the rain, you were fully aware and living in the moment and you were not burdened by your problems. Those are the moments when you are truly living your life rather than *thinking about* your life."

Alex removed the plate of pancakes from the oven and placed the last few on the stack. "Believe it or not, your problems all stem from believing that one or another of those ideas of self represents who you really are."

Dave was shaking his head as they sat down to eat. "I know we discussed this yesterday but I just can't get my head around what you're saying. And I still have real problems—just ask my banker."

"I'm not denying there is a situation which has cost you a lot of money and the result might be you lose your home. What I'm saying is that this doesn't have to be a problem. It becomes a problem for you only when you make a judgment about it. Even if you lose your current home, you're not going to be on the street. You might have to live in a home that's more like what the rest of us have and that will only be a problem if 'Dave the concept' or 'Dave's ego' sees it as a problem.

"The concept of duality might help to explain it. There is a world of events and situations that we cannot change. For example, you can't change the fact that the bank may go after you for the money owed by your company. But for anything to be a problem there must be duality, and that simply means there is the actual situation and there is a 'person' or an 'idea of self' that makes a judgment about it. Basically the judgment is that a different situation would be better."

Alex offered an example. "Here's a real-world situation: say it's pouring rain. Now is that a problem? If I have an idea of myself and I'm aware of my desire to work on the rock wall then the rain is a problem for me because it's uncomfortable to work in the rain and the rocks are slippery. But what about my neighbor Doug, who has recently planted 100 acres of corn? For him the rain is not a problem; it's the answer to a prayer. So the rain itself is not the problem. The 'problem' only arises when there is a 'person' who makes a judgment about it."

Dave thought while he chewed a mouthful of pancake. "Let me get this straight. Are you saying that if the bank petitions me into bankruptcy that's not a problem?"

"I'm saying that for sure it's a *situation* that has to be dealt with. But it's only a *problem* and therefore a source of unhappiness if you perceive it as one. For it to be a problem there has to be judgment. And for judgment there has to be duality. You have, one, the situation and two, the person or idea who wants something to be different. The reality is that you can't change the facts on the ground. Seeing it as a problem doesn't help. All you can do is deal with the facts and the issues efficiently. And you'll do a better job of dealing with the situation if your mind is not distracted and consumed with unproductive 'poor me' and feeling sorry for yourself types of thoughts. The situation is the same; it's just not a problem anymore. Of course you can't change a situation that has already happened."

Alex refilled his coffee. "When I worked as a CA in public practice I had a lot of entrepreneurs as clients. These were guys who took risks and put everything on the line every day. In circles like that, if you haven't gone through bankruptcy once or twice your friends might think you're not fully committed. For this group of individuals, most of whom eventually became very successful, going through bankruptcy was like a rite of passage. It was a time to recalibrate, and there were some consequences that had to be dealt with, but bankruptcy was not perceived as an insurmountable problem."

Alex softened his tone as he reminded his good friend, "You've seen situations, and you've been there yourself, where there were several 'problems'"—here he demonstrated air quotes—"manifesting themselves at the same time, and sometimes there is so much that needs to be done, you become overwhelmed and you can't effectively deal with any one of the problems, let alone all of them at the same time. In these cases, would you not be able to deal with the situation better if you dealt with facts and events in a calm and unemotional way?

"For example," Alex said, taking a couple more pancakes, "have you ever heard one of those recorded conversations between someone calling 911 and the dispatcher? You can hear the sheer panic in the voice of the caller while the dispatcher is very calm and cool—and if the dispatcher acted otherwise then they wouldn't be able to do the job as well."

"Oh, I know it's better to be unemotional when dealing with some problems. The problem is actually doing that."

Alex replied, "I would say you can deal more effectively with any situation if you don't see it as a problem. And if you don't have the 'Dave idea' floating around in your mind, there will be no judgment, as in, this is good or this is bad for Dave. It's that judgment that's required for a situation, one that must be dealt with in the real world, to become a problem."

Seizing onto an idea, Dave asked, "Okay, what about the terrorists who want to blow themselves up and destroy civilization as we know it? Is that not a problem?"

Undeterred, Alex replied, "It's a very real situation, and it has to be dealt with, and given their desire to kill themselves, there's no real possibility of negotiating with them. So to defend our loved ones the best solution may be to identify the enemy, fight them and destroy them. But there is no need to hate them or get emotional about it. We'll do a better job and we'll be more effective if we deal with the situation in an effective and unemotional way."

"Alex my boy, you must have ice running in your veins. Don't you get passionate about anything?"

"Of course I do—just ask my wife. Sometimes I cry during

chick flicks. And the reason I'm likely to cry at movies is because I'm 100 percent into it. I'm totally living in the moment so it's as if I'm there and experiencing the situation myself. When I'm watching a movie I'm not thinking, 'here I am watching a movie.' It's as if I'm *in* the movie. That's why I get so involved.

"Here's another way to look at things. There are natural emotions that stem from pure awareness or consciousness and there are emotions that stem from making a judgment. Let's say you're in a restaurant enjoying your meal. You smell smoke, you see flames and you hear an alarm go off in the kitchen. The natural 'living in pure awareness' response is to get up and run away as fast as you can. When you act in this way you're acting naturally. You're not making judgments about the situation or thinking how stupid the cook was to let a fire start, you're just reacting and running as fast as you can." He glanced across the room. "I turned the stove off, didn't I?"

Seeing that he had, Alex continued with his example. "Later, after the fire is out, you start to think about it, you experience duality—the idea of yourself and the idea of the fire—and then you start to see problems. Now you're the thinker who looks at the situation and makes a judgment about how serious it is. In running out of the restaurant you tore your best trousers and you lost your wallet. That's the situation on the ground. But it doesn't become a *problem* until you abandon the normal 'run away' response and adopt the role of an aggrieved restaurant patron. And in that role you start making judgments."

Smiling, Dave asked, "What's the bottom line? Are you saying you enjoy movies more than I do?"

Alex said, "Yes, unless they're scary movies, which I just can't watch. Do you see my point about the difference between periods of pure awareness versus identifying with the current idea of yourself that's in your mind?"

"Yes, I think so."

"Good." He nodded toward the window." Look—the sun is out and we have work to do. Today we have to take the wheelbarrow further up the line fence and pick up a few flatter rocks we can use to level off the top of the wall."

Dave finished his coffee and they put their dishes in the sink and headed to the back porch. Dave picked up the gloves he had worn yesterday. "These gloves are a bit uncomfortable; I think they're a bit small. I'm going to go without. I've got pretty tough hands."

Alex didn't sound convinced of the wisdom of this decision. "Well, be careful because when your finger gets jammed between a fifty-pound rock and a hard place, it hurts." Once they were outside, Alex said, "You head on down to the end of the line and I'll be with you in a couple of minutes. I've just got to go to the barn to pick up a hammer and stone chisel."

Raising his eyebrows, Dave asked, "What do we need that for? Are we graduating to breaking rocks?"

"Yes—today's new skill is cutting rocks to size! There are a couple of rocks further down the path which are too heavy to lift. But they're sedimentary rocks and are easy to split if you place the chisel along a seam. So we'll split those into smaller flat rocks we can use for the top of the wall."

"I'll walk down with you."

The two got what they needed from the jumble of tools in the barn and then headed toward the pile of stones beyond the end of the wall, a walk of about five minutes. Alex pointed out specific stones to Dave. "Okay here are a couple we can split into smaller, flatter rocks which will be perfect for the top of the wall." He patted one. "Help me roll this on its edge so you can drive the chisel into this crack."

They heaved the large stone a quarter turn. Alex held it on its edge while Dave gave the chisel three sharp blows and the heavy rock separated into two pieces. Dave looked at Alex with a surprised, happy smile.

Looking with approval, Alex said, "See? That part with a two-inch thickness is perfect. Now let's split the bigger section." Dave gave the thicker piece half a dozen sharp blows and it separated again into two slices. "These will be perfect as capping stones," Alex said. "But let's head to the field and get some more."

For the next half hour Alex and Dave were completely absorbed in the task of loading rocks into the wheelbarrow and taking them to the end of the wall.

After the third load, Dave asked, "Alex, can you explain why we're using a wheelbarrow for this? Wouldn't a small backhoe or a tractor make this a lot easier?"

"That will be Phase Two, which will happen when I'm too old and weak to lift a good-sized rock."

After working and thinking for a while Dave said, "So let's say I'm living in, as you call it, this Zen state of pure awareness. What else would be different?"

Alex replied, "Well, first of all, no one lives in pure awareness all the time. We have to function in society and we need to look after ourselves and get to work, get our meals and so on. During the day as we do these things we're going to have many minutes when we're acting and thinking as one would expect based on whatever role we're in—employee, parent, boss, the whole gamut.

"The difference," Alex explained, "is that if you understand the truth of who you really are you're not going to let situations on the ground become big problems. You're just going to deal with them without having to handle all the baggage that comes with different roles and the judgments and problems we create for ourselves in these various roles. You're not going to worry about trying to defend and support the image you currently hold of yourself in your mind.

"Okay," Dave said, "but you're in the business of dealing with wealthy people and helping them manage their money wisely. In that business I'd think that image is quite important. Do you think you'd have many clients if you were not presenting a good image?"

"Oh, I agree, in business image is important. But I think the best image to present would be one of honesty and authenticity. I don't think I'd be a very good actor. So if I was consciously trying to act out the role that I imagined my clients were expecting from me, I think I'd come across as someone who is not being honest." Alex paused to watch what Dave was doing.

"Hold on a second, Dave. I think you need to reposition that last rock you placed. We need a little more batter on this side."

"Batter? What are you talking about?"

"Traditionally a drystone wall slopes slightly inward, and the degree to which it gets narrower at the top is called 'batter.' The usual batter is a rate of about an inch for every six inches of height. So this wall's about three feet high and three feet wide at the base, so it should be about two feet wide at the top. This makes it more esthetically pleasing and also adds to the stability. We don't want to have to rebuild it next year!"

"You got that right. It's enjoyable, but not *that* enjoyable! I'll move this one in a bit. And now I know there's two types of batter." Dave now looked at the wall end-on after he placed each stone, eager to keep the batter right.

Alex continued with his thought after they had worked for a while. "We normally think of ourselves as being separate and unique individuals. But in fact there is a common thread that binds us and makes us all part of a larger whole. Nisargadatta was a famous Yogi teacher and to explain this point he used the example of a drop of spray which might have been blown off the top of a huge ocean wave. If that drop of spray could think, it might think, 'here I am flying through the air, isn't this great!'

A few seconds later the drop of spray falls back into the ocean and once again becomes an indistinguishable part of the vast ocean. In somewhat the same way, for a brief time humans appear to be separate individuals, but then we die and we are once again part of the universal life force.

"The objective in Raja Yoga and Zen is really the same. In Yoga they call it achieving Nirvana, or self-realization, but it's really about discovering the same truth by a slightly different method. In Zen we're not trying to describe perfectly who we are, because our minds are not great enough to understand the universe. All we're trying to do is identify those ideas that are clearly false, those that make us think we're someone we're not and which are a source of problems in our lives. By eliminating the problems that come from misunderstanding who we are, we can enjoy more happiness and enjoy life to the fullest." Alex picked up a fairly small rock and wedged it into a gap that it filled perfectly.

"When I stop identifying with and worrying about this aging body," Alex went on, "there is greater awareness of my true essence, which is more than the ideas I have of myself. I'm not suggesting that we not look after our bodies. You know I go to the gym and eat healthy foods, and I try not to drink to excess. Although I do love the advice 'moderation in all things—including moderation!' That's the philosophy that enables old friends to have a few additional drinks after a hard day of moving rocks."

Dave piped up, "That part I can agree with, with no reservations!"

A moment later Dave let out a yelp and danced around holding the index finger of his right hand tightly in his left hand. He opened his hand to inspect the damage and then walked over to show the bruised finger to Alex.

"Yup," Alex said, "that fingernail will be turning black and you'll be losing it. It's just one of the hazards of building with stone. Maybe you should reconsider the gloves."

A smile spreading over his face, Dave said, "But I'm sure you have lots of liability insurance! So maybe I'll be able to solve my financial problems after all!"

Alex laughed. "Yes, for sure. Anyway, it's almost lunchtime so we can go back and put that on ice for a bit. But back to what I was saying; having a drink with a friend reminds us that Zen is about enjoying life. We can't avoid growing old and eventually dying, but knowing who we really are can help us live life to the fullest."

Moving to the last stone that Dave had laid and testing it to see that it didn't wobble, Alex continued. "There's a delightful story about a Zen monk who was being chased by a tiger. The monk ran as fast as he could but the tiger was getting closer. Finally the monk avoided the tiger by climbing over a ledge. He hung onto some vines to save himself from falling to another ledge thirty feet below. While hanging on he noticed that another tiger was pacing on the ledge below, waiting for him to fall. When he looked back up he saw that mice were eating away at the vines and he knew he only had a short time before they gnawed the vines through and he would fall to his death. Looking around, he noticed a few juicy ripe strawberries growing within his reach. He reached over and picked them and said 'mmm…what a tasty treat.'" Alex placed another stone.

"There are a few points to this story. One, the monk didn't just lie down and let the tiger kill him. He ran as fast as he could to save his life. While running, it's safe to assume he was paying full attention to his running. He was not thinking of himself and what might happen to him, he was in the zone and was fully focused on the path and the tiger and this allowed him to run as fast as possible.

"And even while hanging from the vine he was enjoying life

to the fullest. Although certain death awaited him below he used his remaining minutes to enjoy the strawberries. He couldn't have done this if he was thinking about himself. Although he did his very best to preserve his life, he was not worried about losing it because he understood what part of his life was real and what part was only a concept. In Zen we would say the monk had lost his life a long time ago. This happened at the moment he came to the realization that the idea he had of himself was false. He was able to enjoy the strawberries because, having realized that the concept he held in his mind was false, he knew there was nothing more to lose."

Alex looked at Dave. "Isn't that a great story? It illustrates enjoying every moment of life, right up to the very end."

Dave protested. "But he had his life to lose! He's not going to be doing anything after he falls thirty feet and the tiger eats him."

"True. But let me say a couple of things about that and then let's get lunch. My first point is that the monk did everything he possibly could to avoid death. But death will come to us all. In the last few moments of his life he had two choices: he could enjoy a tasty treat or he could curse his bad luck. He's dead either way. Don't you agree, the best way to enjoy life is to enjoy every moment?"

"I guess that makes sense."

"The second point is that if you've given up all your false ideas of self then there is no image of 'Dave' in your mind to experience either business failure or death. You can't experience mental suffering unless you have duality—the idea of yourself and the idea of what you want to be different.

"When you're dreaming, everything seems real, but when you wake up you know it was a dream. Lying in bed, you are absolutely certain that the real you is different from the mental image you had of yourself in your dream. Well, when you fully grasp this idea that Dave is a concept—in the same way that the 'university' is a concept—you'll have the same level of certainty about knowing that the real you is more than the idea you have in your mind at any given moment."

Dave nodded. "Okay; that's something to look forward to. And I can see that this all could be true and it would be nice to be able to go through life enjoying every minute regardless of, as you call them, the situations on the ground."

Alex smiled. "You should also understand that I didn't come up with these ideas on my own. I'm just giving you a quick overview of what Zen practitioners have discovered during the 2,500 year history of searching for understanding about who we really are. And I'm not saying it's easy, but with a Zen practice you can get to the point where you're not overly concerned about the ideas you have of yourself because you've discovered that the 'person' who creates all the ideas doesn't even exist as you seem to exist."

Dave shook his head. "Okay, I know you believe this stuff. And I really can't argue with you because it sort of makes sense. But for most people, particularly older people like my parents, you might as well be talking in a foreign language. They have worries because they see themselves running out of money and ending their days in a ward in some government nursing home. I can't tell them, 'don't worry, you don't exist.' I know they shouldn't be worried because they have their home and over a million dollars. But for people in their age group, dipping into one's capital is seen as a slippery slope leading to certain disaster. Do you have any...kind of non-Zen ideas that will convince them that they're not going to run out of money and they should start to enjoy life while they still have good health?"

Alex said, "For most people like your parents the solution is quite simple and it's all about common sense; there's no need to talk about anything except common-sense ideas. What they need is a financial plan that lays out the numbers in a clear and simple way. A proper financial plan will prove to them beyond any reasonable doubt that they have enough and then I think they will be able to enjoy life more."

Dave said, "Okay I want to hear about this. But we have to eat lunch—and I think I may need a glass of wine!" Dave was still nursing his finger so Alex gathered up their tools and gloves and they walked to the house. As they were walking Dave said, "Here's a question: would a practitioner of Zen want a financial plan?"

"A properly prepared financial plan is like a road map. It tells you the easiest way, in financial terms, to get from A to B, but—and this is the important point—you have to know where you want to go. If you know what your financial goals are, the plan shows you what you have to do to achieve your objective. A Zen master is not interested in amassing a fortune, but a financial plan might be worthwhile because it could show where next month's food and shelter are coming from and this might allow him to do more for his students.

"Notice that it's taking a few more steps to get to the house?" Alex observed. "That proves the wall is longer now! The main variables in a financial plan are how much you expect to earn, how much you want to spend, how much you plan to save, how long you're going to work and what the real rate of return on your investments will be. The real rate of return is the rate of return over and above inflation. Of course that will depend on the asset mix and the level of risk you are exposed to.

"In terms of achieving financial goals and removing financial worries" Alex concluded, "I really can't think of anything more important than a properly prepared financial plan."

As they entered the back porch and took off their shoes, Alex added, "I remember one of my clients who was retired and living on a low fixed income. But she enjoyed financial security because, although she didn't have a lot coming in each month, she had a financial plan and she knew the amount that was coming in was more than what was going out. So she was confident she was going to be okay. Her financial plan included the one-time cost of a luxury cruise, which she and her sister had planned to take when they were both retired. When her sister finally retired they went on the trip.

"Her sister was a widow and she had almost $2 million in investments, much of which had come from an insurance policy on her deceased husband. Although this woman was wealthy she didn't have a financial plan and she didn't know how much she would need in order to maintain her lifestyle for the next thirty years. Without a plan she worried about every dollar she spent. During the cruise she complained constantly: 'Look at the cost of this' and 'Oh dear, I'm afraid we're going to rue the day we took this expensive cruise.' My client had less money but she had confidence she would be okay because she had a sound financial plan that showed that she could afford the trip. She enjoyed every minute of it. Her sister, who had more money but no plan, was miserable and her money was wasted because her worries outweighed the pleasure."

Alex and Dave scrubbed up in the kitchen sink while Alex explained, "The thing is, if you have a financial plan that shows you can spend $50,000 per year, there is no need to worry unless you spend more than $50,000. Someone who has the same amount of money invested, but who doesn't know what their safe spending limit is, will worry about every dollar they spend—even when their spending is within the sustainable limit—because they don't know what that limit is.

"Usually for the first draft of a financial plan people don't know what to expect. But when they see how things are supposed to work out based on the initial assumptions, then they can ask, 'What if I work longer? What if I spend less? Or if we buy or sell a house or if I retire sooner? What if we get a higher or lower rate of return?' etc., etc. With Millennials I like to show them the difference spending a couple of hundred dollars less each month can make. When they see that doing that could mean being able to buy a home or vacation property, educating their children or retiring two to five years sooner, they become savers rather than spenders!"

Alex gripped the handle of the fridge but finished his thought before opening it. "For very wealthy people I use the financial plan to help them to decide, A, what the required rate of return is to achieve their goals and B, how to feel more comfortable giving more money away, and have fun doing it, while they're living. Most people don't have the goal of leaving their children with so much money they'll never have to work. So the only sensible alternative is to give it away while you're still living, because to the best of my knowledge, no one takes it with them when they die.

"The problem is that without a financial plan that maps out the worst-case scenarios, wealthy people don't know how much money they need. The result is that they don't get to enjoy their money. Trust me, the money will get spent by someone, but that may not be the people who earned it."

Sunday afternoon.

Control, consequences and guilt

Alex opened the fridge and looked in. "Looks like we have three choices for lunch. We have beef stew left over from last night, or we can make sandwiches—there's sliced meat, or I could do a 'Frank special.' That would be a salad with baby romaine, bell peppers, English cucumber, avocado, chicken, pepitas and balsamic-olive oil dressing. It comes with a caramelized sweet onion and old cheddar omelet."

"Wow. And you just happen to have all that stuff in the fridge? Sounds good, though," Dave said. "Who's Frank? Is he a chef?"

"No, he's just one of the guys who comes to the annual medical retreat. You should come to the next retreat and you'll get to meet him."

Dave pulled from the fridge the bottle of wine he had brought with him. "I think this Riesling would go really well with a Frank special. Do you need some help to make it? Sounds involved."

"Nope, I'm good. You pour the wine and I'll make the salad."

"Really—I could grate the cheese or something."

"Okay, yes, you could grate the cheese. And maybe slice the onions."

"I thought so," Dave laughed. He poured them both a glass of wine and set to work beside Alex. Soon the fragrance of caramelizing onions filled the kitchen.

When everything was chopped, Alex assembled the salads on two large plates and beat the eggs for the omelet. As he swirled the eggs in the pan, Dave refilled their wine glasses. As they sat down to begin their lunch, Dave asked, "Alex, are you ready for another important question?"

"Fire away."

Collecting his thoughts, Dave started, "Okay. I sort of vaguely understand what you're saying about me not existing in exactly the way I think I do, particularly given that I've been changing my opinion of myself lately. But if that's the case, then my wife also doesn't exist and my children don't exist and I don't want to hear this because I love my wife and children."

Alex nodded. "You're raising a couple of good points. But first, I've never said that you or anyone else doesn't exist. We know that physically, we all exist. All I'm really saying is that you should try to identify with the part of you which is constant and true and has never changed. This unchangeable part (since birth) is your sense of presence, your consciousness, your awareness when you're so focused on something that you forget who you are. I'm saying that you should recognize as false all the different ideas you have of yourself at different times of the day. Also, and this is the hard part, understand that when you come to realize that all the ideas you have of yourself are false, you'll also discover that the thinker who makes this realization is also false. So that's point number one."

Dave nodded. "Okay."

"The next point is to understand is why we love someone. Our first and most natural love is to love ourselves. If we didn't have this as a natural instinct we wouldn't have survived as a species. We also naturally love our children and I believe that's because we see ourselves in our children. Loving our children is an extension of loving ourselves.

"But the love for a spouse is different. We love our spouse

because we love how we feel when we're with them. Being with our spouse makes us feel complete, secure and happy. If things change and our spouse makes us feel threatened, frustrated, angry or unhappy then our love ceases or could even turn to hate. Love for a spouse is about the fulfillment of our desires, whether the desire is for companionship, financial security, sex, friendship or to make ourselves feel complete."

Confused, Dave asked, "So are you saying that if I saw Judy as she really is and if I didn't have an illusion about who I was, then I'd have no reason to love her?"

"No. I'm saying that you could then love her differently, because your ego or the false sense you have of who you are wouldn't be jumping in and demanding attention. And Judy would love you more because you wouldn't be so stubborn and hard to get along with and you wouldn't be so needy. Sometimes people feel they're in love with someone because that someone satisfies their needs. But this is often a temporary fix because our needs change and ultimately your partner will never be able to satisfy all your needs. Ultimately you have to make yourself happy. You can't always depend on someone else to satisfy your needs and make you happy.

"With regard to the incorrect understanding of who you really are: if you and Judy are like most people, more than half your disagreements are the result of hurt feelings or pride and feeling the need to defend a damaged ego. And hurt feelings and damaged egos are always to do with the false image of self currently being held in your mind."

Dave smiled, "Yes, I know Judy has all these flaws!"

Acknowledging Dave's comment with a smile, Alex carried on. "If you understand your true essence and you understand that the ideas you have of yourself, including the idea that you exist as a separate individual, and here I'm not talking about physical body, are all false, then not only will you be more loveable to your spouse but you can also have greater love for all humanity.

"The Bible urges us to love one another as we love ourselves. This is because the love of self is the strongest love. But as long as you see other people as separate and different it's difficult to love them quite as much as you love yourself. However, if you recognize that all people share the same true essence, and you can therefore see yourself in other people, and you recognize that the differences are superficial and unimportant, then it's easy to love another as you love yourself—or at least be more patient and understanding!"

"Okay, I think I'm still with you—but you have to agree this is pretty heavy stuff for this early in the day. This is a fantastic salad, by the way. This Frank guy knows what's going on."

"Thank you," Alex nodded. "The problem for most people is that they have the wrong idea of who they are, and they have the wrong idea of who the other person is, and because both entities are described according to physical characteristics, occupations or beliefs that they hold, the differences may seem very great. When we focus on differences it's hard to love other people because differences represent threats to our ideas and values. On the other hand, when you see, through the study of Zen, that all the ideas you have about yourself and about other people are false, and you become aware of the truth of who you really are, then you're more likely to focus on similarities rather than differences."

"Alex, you missed your calling. You should have been a preacher!"

"I thought about it; but that's another story. As I said, with family, children and close friends, there can also be an intense and natural love, and it is based on the perception of similarities. We love our family because they are part of us. We love our friends because they share experiences and they seem to be like us in many ways. The point is that when we focus more on what we have in common, and less on the differences between ourselves and others, it becomes easier to be tolerant of the differences."

Dave started to counter this but stopped, giving a nod to show he saw the truth of it. But he let out a long breath. "Okay, approaching mind-blowout. I need another glass of wine!" He divided the last of the wine between their glasses.

"Me too; I get excited when I have a chance to talk to someone who is willing to listen to what I have to say!"

They remained at the table for a time while they finished their wine. While Alex took the bottle out to the recycling bin, Dave filled the sink. By the time they had finished the dishes, it had started to rain.

Alex said, "Looks like that's the end of our wall building for this weekend. I'm not a fan of working in the rain."

"I'm a bit tired out anyway. I'm not used to slinging heavy rocks around," Dave replied. He held up his bruised finger and smiled. "And don't forget—I'm injured. I don't mind taking it easy this afternoon. I have to head back this afternoon anyway—I told Judy I'd be home for dinner. Although I don't like the idea of driving in this downpour."

"So let's just relax and I'll put on a pot of coffee."

"Sounds good," Dave said. "And since we're sitting around waiting for the rain to stop, I think I may have a few more questions I'd like your Zen response to."

"Fire away." Alex leaned on the kitchen counter while they waited for the coffee to brew.

Dave got mugs from the cupboard and set them on the counter. He took a deep breath. "So here's one: if the truth be known, I feel a bit guilty about what happened to my business because I took my eye off the ball over the last year. I was starting to get bored and I was hanging out with a bunch of guys who were already retired. We played a lot of golf and we curled in the winter, and we had long lunches. It felt like I was only in the office half the time and sometimes I wasn't really thinking clearly after those long lunches. The worst part is, I brought Don into the business and assigned him responsibility for tasks that he wasn't remotely prepared for—things I should have been doing. Now that the business is essentially gone, *he* feels responsible. And I feel absolutely terrible about that. Maybe you know of a way I can think about this that will…I don't know, give me another perspective."

Alex poured their coffee. "I can empathize." He motioned toward the back of the house. "Let's get comfortable." They went to the family room. "I understand how badly you must feel. So it's important that you understand what I am going to tell you about guilt and regret. Like everything else there is a Zen way of thinking about this that can help.

"I might even light a fire," Alex said as they entered the family room. "It's not that warm." He set about building a small fire in the fireplace. "First of all, there is the real-world situation: your business has collapsed. The amount of guilt you feel or don't feel isn't going to change that. Nothing is made better by you spending the rest of your life feeling guilty. In fact, it only makes things worse, because if your son is accepting some of the responsibility for how things turned out, seeing you feel guilty is only going to make him feel worse."

With the fire going, Alex sat down in the armchair. "Let's use my standard approach. By now you should have a good idea what my next question will be."

"You're going to ask what idea I'm entertaining about myself when I feel guilty. In short, who feels guilty?"

"Exactly. Right now you have an idea in your mind in which you're playing the role of business guy who screwed up. That idea probably alternates with the idea of a father who let his son down. Consider this example: since you may soon be looking for work, imagine you take a job as a playwright." Dave guffawed, which made Alex laugh too. "Bear with me. Some small theater company is *really* desperate and they hire you to write a play about an architect who screws up by designing an office building that collapses and kills scores of people. Of course the play's a flop and you move on to another job, one you can actually do. While you're working at your new job are you going to feel any pangs of guilt for the architect you created in your play? No, of course not; that architect was only an idea, he wasn't real. I imagine you see where I'm going from here?"

Dave grudgingly replied, "Okay, I get it. You're going to say that all the guilt I feel is associated with an image I have of myself in my mind and then you're going to say that the image is no more real than the architect. You're going to say I'm not the idea, I'm the life force that creates the environment for that idea to occur. How did I do?"

Applauding, Alex exclaimed, "You really were listening! Now my only question is whether you're just repeating it or whether you really believe it."

Dave thought for a moment. "Let's say I'm still trying to get my head around it." He hoisted his mug. "Caffeine may help."

Alex continued enthusiastically. "On Friday we started this conversation by talking about happiness. Feelings of guilt and regret are just a type of desire that brings unhappiness. In this case it's the impossible desire to change something that happened in the past, wishing that something we did could be undone or wishing we could go back and do something we failed to do. One way to eliminate feelings of guilt is to have a better understanding of responsibility and consequences. Every action has consequences and we have to accept the consequences of our actions and behavior. But guilt is a totally unnecessary feeling. It doesn't change what's already happened. And it's also wrong, because guilt suggests that you had complete control over the event. Sometimes, simply by understanding that you weren't in control, you'll stop feeling guilty. You can still empathize, just as we feel sympathy for the victims of an earthquake or flood, but we don't feel guilty about it because we know we weren't responsible for the disaster."

"I get the earthquake thing, but I think my own business is a pretty different case. Or are you now going to say that I didn't have as much control as I thought I did, or that as the owner of the business my control was only an idea?"

"In every situation, we all take the action which seems to make the most sense given our personality and our understanding of the circumstances. We all do the same thing; some people have better information and make better decisions, but we all do the best we can with what we have to work with at the time. If you understand this principle you'll never have feelings of guilt again. Marie no longer asks me why I did something which in hindsight seems quite dumb. The answer is always the same: at the time, based on my information and the only ideas that came to mind, it seemed like the best course of action."

"That's a good line," Dave replied. "I'm going to remember that one."

Alex got up to get more coffee but added before he went to the kitchen, "Individuals who think they're in control and who think they are personally responsible for their decisions, and therefore deserve praise or blame, vastly underestimate the innumerable factors that contribute to the outcome of any situation. The causes of an event, a car accident for example, can be traced back to absurd levels. Say you're late for an important meeting. You're speeding along and you have an accident. Are you to blame because you were in a hurry? Is your son to blame because you lost time filling up with gas because he forgot to do it? Is your wife to blame because she delayed you with some domestic chore? Is your mechanic to blame for failing to replace worn brakes? Is your father to blame for drilling into you that it's disrespectful to be late for a meeting? One could go on indefinitely coming up with the names of individuals who, if they had behaved differently, could have caused you to behave differently and avoid the accident." He reached for Dave's mug. "Coffee?" Dave handed the cup up to him.

When he returned from the kitchen, Alex concluded his thought. "None of this in any way suggests that there is a way to avoid the consequences of an action. Right or wrong, fair or unfair, there are consequences for every action and it is wise to accept and live with those consequences. But this is different from feeling guilty about some action we took. Consequences we should accept. Feelings of guilt are unnecessary and should never be accepted." A low rumble of thunder caused both Dave and Alex to turn toward the window.

Continuing the conversation, Dave said, "But I can think of dozens of small things that if I'd done them a bit differently or a bit sooner, my problems could have been avoided and I'd be feeling great right now."

"As they say on TV, wait—there's more. What I just said was the good part. Here's the part that might not seem so good. I know you've enjoyed the feeling of success that you've had up until recently and you felt pride in what you've accomplished. But the reality is that just as there is no reason to feel guilty over things that didn't turn out as planned, there's no reason to feel pride in the things that did work out as planned."

"So the guilt-free life was too good to be true, huh?"

Undeterred, Alex continued. "There are three points on this and again, you know what the first is going to be."

Dave nodded. "You're going to say that the idea of myself when I'm accepting praise is not the real me, and you'll probably also say that just as the failed architect in my non-award-winning play deserves no blame, he—and I—also deserve no praise. Because we're just ideas."

Smiling and nodding, Alex said, "Right. That's my first point. My second point is that just as there were innumerable things that contributed to the failure of the business, there were innumerable things that contributed to your success in building it. Without these things it is unlikely that you would have been successful. You were born in Canada to good parents who taught you values and a strong work ethic. You inherited good genes and you were born with high intelligence. You grew up next to good neighbors and were part of a community that gave you positive role models, and you grew up in a town where the schools had some of the best teachers in the country. Now is there any part of that which you can really take credit for? You did nothing to earn this or deserve this good start in life—you were just lucky! A number of experts have confirmed that if you want success the most important first step is to choose your parents wisely!"

Dave protested, "Okay, fine, but what about cases where two children from the same family turn out completely different? It would seem that they had the same advantages or disadvantages—shouldn't the one who has done better deserve some credit?"

"I think it's impossible," Alex said, "to know all the things that can make a difference in a person's life." He got up to jostle the logs in the fireplace. "There's something a wealthy client once told me that I found quite interesting. When I was in public practice as a CPA, this client owned a very successful car dealership. I knew he had grown up in a rough neighborhood without a lot of opportunities. He had a twin brother who, although a very nice individual, had not achieved the same level of financial security. One time I asked my client how he explained the difference in financial success between himself and his brother, when to all appearances they had the same advantages or disadvantages growing up.

"Fred told me he knew exactly what the difference was. He said he clearly remembered that one day he was sitting on a bench outside a store when a man drove up in a shiny new convertible. It was the nicest car Fred had ever seen. As the man got out and went into the store Fred noticed that he was dressed in a sharp-looking suit and he looked happy and successful. Later Fred asked the shopkeeper who the man was and he was told that he was a businessman who owned an interest in an automobile dealership. At that moment Fred decided he wanted to be successful just like that man driving the shiny new convertible. With that goal in mind he worked as hard as was necessary to become successful.

"Now anyone who knew Fred and his brother would assume they had almost exactly the same advantages, or lack thereof, but they could not know of this turning point in Fred's life—and this is what gave him an edge. But he did nothing to deserve this edge, he was just sitting there when the car drove up. So that's why I'm saying there are innumerable factors that can lead to success or failure and therefore it's wrong when 'you' feel guilt or pride."

Taking a sip of coffee, Dave said, "Fair enough. I agree I had a lot of advantages. But I could have totally screwed my life up. We saw a lot of kids at university who bombed out because they drank too much or didn't study—they threw away the opportunity."

"Sure, but I would say that those kids maybe didn't have the benefit of parents who taught them values, a work ethic and to accept responsibility, as we did. My third point is to bring us back to what we chatted about Friday night, and that was conditional happiness. Although conditional happiness is good, it can change to conditional unhappiness, as it has for you because of your business loss. And that's why a more reliable source of happiness is the unconditional kind, where you're happy, not because you got something you wanted, but because you know how to live in the moment free from any false ideas about the real you."

Alex and Dave sipped their coffee in silence for a few minutes.

Collecting his thoughts, Dave said, "You know, I think I get some of what you're saying. As I now understand it, a Zen practitioner could be successful in business or fail in business and be equally happy either way."

Alex nodded and said, "Yes. Yes, in theory, that's correct. The goal of Zen is to understand who you really are. That will help you to enjoy life whether you're a parent looking after your child, a business owner or the president of the United States. But in reality everyone enjoys some conditional happiness when good things—like a successful business—happen. Even the Zen masters I know can be disappointed when bad things happen. The important difference is that they get over it quickly."

Dave got up and went to the window and watched the rain. After a few minutes, he said, "I have to say, I'm feeling like I understand more about myself and I think I'm going to find a way to get through this and be happy even if I'm never wealthy again. I've got Judy. I've got the family." He turned to face Alex. "I've got true friends. Still, looking back I do feel responsible and I wish I had made some different choices."

Alex smiled. "Of course there are consequences to the decisions you made. But—and this will probably not come as a surprise—I have some thoughts about taking responsibility."

"Yes, let me guess: your first question will be which one of my ideas of myself is going to take responsibility for my choices?"

"Correct. That would be the first question. But let's be clear, for practical purposes we all believe we have freedom of choice. And our laws and courts would seem to confirm that we have freedom of choice. Otherwise, why would we punish people for breaking the law if they had no choice? But you can enjoy more happiness and less regret if you understand the issue better. For example, if you faced a difficult decision and you made the wrong choice, it helps if you realize that you really had no choice but to choose the course of action that you did. If you understand this, it is easier to be happy or at least accept the outcome. The real unhappiness comes when you believe you could have made a better choice. It is on these occasions that you relive the experience, going over it again and again and regretting the decisions you made. Regretting a decision is a waste of time; it's the impossible desire to change what has already happened."

"You can't turn back time, that's for sure." Dave sat back down on the couch.

Alex said, "Feelings of guilt and unhappiness often come from the mistaken view that we have freedom of choice. Of course we often *appear* to have freedom of choice but in reality the choices available to us, and our understanding of those choices, are a result of things over which we have no control and therefore no choice." A log shifted in the fireplace, sending a brief torrent of sparks up the chimney. "If you had grown up in difficult circumstances, and you lived in a neighborhood where you felt you had to join a gang to survive, the options you would have been able to consider and choose from would have been very different from the choices you actually had."

Alex finished his coffee. "I remember when I was studying for my CPA exam, I looked out my window and was envious of the people enjoying the spring weather while I was stuck inside studying. Then it occurred to me that I was actually doing what I wanted to do. I didn't *have* to study for my exam, I wanted to. I knew I would benefit from the completion of the program, and when I weighed the expected enjoyment of that against the presumed enjoyment of being outside on a nice spring day, I chose the path that would give me the greatest happiness. When I realized I was inside studying because that would ultimately give me the greatest happiness, I became content with my choice to study.

"Seems logical," Dave said.

"I now recognize that I appeared to make a choice and then became happier by understanding it, but in reality, given my upbringing and the things my parents taught me, my sense of responsibility to my family, my competitiveness and my understanding of the options, I really had no choice but to make the decision that I did. Understanding this point helps you eliminate feelings of guilt and regret."

Thunder rumbled again, far off. Dave said, "It looks like the rain is not going to let up.

"This talk of what your parents taught you reminds me that I wanted to ask you for your view on my parents' situation. One thing that's happened is that their advisor retired and they don't really like her replacement."

"Right. I can start by giving you copies of some of my articles on investing for retirees but we can also go over their specific situation. One problem I frequently see, and you've said this is a problem your parents have as well, is that they're afraid to spend their money because they don't have a financial plan that demonstrates that they're going to be okay. Another common problem for retirees is that they confuse 'income' with 'cash flow.' Retirees need a certain amount of cash flow every month to maintain their lifestyle but sometimes they think this means they need investments that pay this amount in interest or dividends. The mistake is to fail to recognize that in the investing world 'income' consists of interest, dividends and capital gains. If retirees think the income is only interest and dividends and they design their portfolio to earn only interest and dividends, then they'll not have sufficient diversification.

"To protect themselves against all risks, retirees should have a well-diversified, goals-based portfolio. This is one that would include investments that are expected to earn capital gains as well as interest and dividends. They then create the cash flow they need by using the interest and dividends they've collected and by selling some investments that produce capital gains. This is the best way to create an investment portfolio that provides protection against inflation and is also income tax efficient. I use this approach to help retirees invest and manage their wealth in a way that's consistent with my view that everyone should enjoy life to the fullest."

Dave was quick to say, "Somehow I'm not surprised."

Alex laughed and carried on. "And people like your parents who follow this strategy and others who have even greater wealth find that this approach allows them to enjoy their wealth and increase their happiness."

"Sounds logical enough."

"You might be surprised to know how many wealthy people really don't enjoy the opportunity that's at their fingertips. For these individuals I first try to help them clarify their goals and when goals are clear the next step is to design the portfolio's asset mix so that it can be expected to earn the rate of return necessary to achieve their goals while taking the least possible risk."

"I believe that's easier said than done—isn't it?" Dave asked.

"No, it doesn't have to be complicated. So for those individuals who have far more money than they need to maintain their lifestyle for the rest of their lives, I like to get them to talk about what they believe could possibly make them even happier. Without even getting into any kind of philosophical discussion I can say that in my experience the happiest people on the planet are the ones who spend a lot of time helping others. One reason people are happier when they help others is that while they're doing that they're not thinking about themselves and the things *they* want, right? Because as we discussed before, unfulfilled desires are the source of all unhappiness, and you can only have unfulfilled desires when you're thinking about the things you want. When you're focused on helping someone else you stop thinking about yourself."

Dave stood and picked up the two empty coffee cups. "Well, I can imagine that could be an interesting conversation. What are you likely to learn from it?"

Alex followed Dave to the kitchen. "What I learn is not as important as what retirees and wealthy individuals can learn about themselves. Quite often, after clarifying goals and looking at the investment portfolio two things become obvious. First, they have the opportunity to have more happiness if they spend or give away some of their money before they die, and secondly, there is a major disconnect between the objective for the portfolio and the investments in the portfolio. Then we have a discussion in which we try to uncover the reasons the investment portfolio is inconsistent with how it should be diversified, given their goals.

"One of the topics," Alex continued, "that almost always comes up as a major concern of wealthy people is whether or not a large inheritance will have a positive or negative impact on their children. I don't have the statistics but my experience tells me that unless it's handled properly, a boatload of cash is more likely to cause a negative rather than a positive result for the heirs. So I always recommend clients read a book called *Willing Wisdom*, which provides absolutely the best advice for families where a sizable inheritance is possible."

"I guess the Bradleys don't need a copy just at the moment," Dave said wryly.

"Will you stop?" Alex laughed. "Read it anyway. It's about

making the right decisions so that inherited wealth will help the next generation rather than harm it."

"Okay, I'll look out for it," Dave said as he looked out the kitchen window. "Looks like the rain is backing off a bit. I should get myself organized to go fairly soon. Anything else for the parents?"

"I don't know if this applies to your parents or not, but I know that many people like them spend a lot of time and money and energy developing complicated estate plans primarily designed to reduce income tax. In my view this is a waste of energy if one doesn't first address the important issues about how the money will eventually be used, either spent, given to heirs or given to charity. As *Willing Wisdom* explains, people should first become clear on the purpose of the money and then the rest will fall into place quite easily.

"When I'm dealing with wealthy people I point out that people can be both happy and rich but you need to"—Alex counted on his fingers—"one, become clear on your goals; two, understand that an investment portfolio is simply a tool to achieve your goals; three, get the performance information necessary to manage your money wisely; and four, understand what makes for a happy life. I stress that an investment portfolio is only useful if it helps achieve your goals. If investors think their portfolio has some other use, they will focus too much attention on the portfolio and not enough on what the portfolio can and should be used for."

Dave said, "I can see that."

"Without a clear purpose for the portfolio, and without confidence that it's being managed wisely, a large investment portfolio can be a source of worry. As an example, I recently spoke to one individual who owns a mansion in the Bahamas but when he looks out over the magnificent view of the harbor he doesn't enjoy it because he's constantly wondering if he should be doing something different with his investments.

"It's really sad," Alex said, "that so many wealthy investors waste so much time and energy thinking about the wrong investment issues. One reason for this is that without that performance report I keep talking about, one that points out the real problems that need to be addressed, investors don't know what they should or should not be worried about. But with proper reports they can have confidence that their portfolio is being well managed to achieve their goals and they can stop worrying about their portfolio and start enjoying life. And, if the report shows they're not on track and their advisors are not adding value, then they know what to do to correct the problem."

"And there we are, back to not worrying," Dave noted. "I'm going to go up and grab my stuff."

When Dave came back downstairs with his bag, Alex was emerging from the den with a file folder. Dave set his bag by the door to the back porch and took the file when Alex offered it to him. "These," Alex said, "are the articles I mentioned, for the kids and your folks."

"Thanks a million," Dave said as he flipped through the pages. "This looks like it will give them an excellent foundation."

"I do get into some of the nuts and bolts of investing when I talk to people like your parents," Alex continued. "I like to explain how investors with large portfolios should stop thinking about investments and the things they can't control and start to think more about things they can control, such as the best way to spend or give away the capital they've accumulated.

"Some of these questions are answered by having a financial plan that shows what has to be done to achieve goals and an estimate of the size of the estate that will be left over. For wealthy retired people," Alex said, "one of the most difficult challenges is to become clear on the best way to use the capital they've accumulated.

"Dave, for people who have more money than they need to maintain their desired lifestyle, I explain that they can have a lot of fun if they start today to give more money to family members or the charitable causes they support. Philanthropists give their money away while they're living because they have fun doing it. Helping others creates happiness in two ways: first, there is the good feeling from being recognized by your community, and secondly, there is the happiness that comes because when you're helping others you're not thinking about your own problems. In other words, you're living in the moment. And as we know," he smiled, "this is the key to happiness."

Dave said, "This makes a lot of sense—I wish I still had a large investment portfolio, because if I did, I'd have a lot of fun giving it away!" He picked up his bag and Alex followed him out into the light rain.

"When we understand the rules of any sport and recognize a great move when we see one, we get more enjoyment from watching a game. Similarly, when we understand the source of happiness, and when we recognize our many opportunities for happiness, we can be happier and spend more time living in the moment.

"So those are some of the points I make to help wealthy people manage their money and maximize their happiness. And what's the result of failure to take charge and actually use up capital in a way that will maximize one's happiness? There'll be a larger estate—and the heirs will have more money to spend. And there's nothing wrong with that if it's what the individual wants. But if maximizing their children's happiness is the goal, there may be a better way. In many cases the better way is to give money to the children in stages through their twenties, thirties and forties so they can use it to help achieve their personal and career goals. This gives them an opportunity to make their mistakes and learn wealth management skills. It also gives parents an opportunity to assess whether or not the funds are being used responsibly."

The two friends walked out to Dave's truck. They hugged and Dave got into the truck and opened the window to continue the conversation.

"Percy Ross," Alex said, "who gave away millions, was quoted as saying, 'he who gives while he lives also knows where it goes!'"

Dave smiled. "Well, it will be a while before I have a chance to have the pleasure of giving money away. But here's good news: with regard to the decision about the business, I've decided I don't need to do anything. As you've explained, there is a situation with my business but it's not a problem unless I make it a problem. And I've decided not to make this a problem. I see now that it only becomes a problem when I put one of my hats on and adopt one or another of the roles I customarily adopt. So I'm going to tell my potential buyer I really don't care which way it goes. I'll deal with whatever situation presents itself and I'm not going to let my ego get involved. I suspect that what will happen is that I'll get a better price and I'll sell—and then enjoy working there as an employee. Otherwise I'll mortgage the house and put the money into the business. And I'll be fine either way because I really see that it's the idea I have of myself that's going to do well or do poorly. And if I don't like what's happened to my current idea of Dave as the businessman, maybe I'll see myself in a different role—maybe as Dave the drystone wall builder!

"Alex, this has been a great weekend. I'm going to be driving back home feeling better than I did on the way down here, and that really was what I was hoping for. I think I understood some of what you explained; I'm certainly going to try to stop thinking negative thoughts and stop seeing myself as a failure."

Alex responded, "Good. Good, I'm glad to hear it. But I want you to understand that the objective in Zen is not to replace wrong and negative ideas of self with wrong but positive ideas of self. The objective in Zen is to realize that *all* ideas you have of yourself as an individual are wrong. Remember the 'university' example. It's the same with the concept of self. You have a physical body and a mind and a history and experience and then you tie it together and add the concept of 'Dave.' Adding in the concept of 'Dave' is the part that's wrong; just remember that."

Alex continued, "If you really want to learn more I'll send you a list of a few books which I've found very helpful. You could even try a few classes in meditation. Every city has centers where they offer meditation and the best way to acquire this self-knowledge is to start meditating under the supervision of someone who knows what they're talking about."

"Well, we'll see. But I am determined to work at it until I better understand who I really am."

Smiling, Alex said, "Actually, while determination to be successful works when you're starting a business, it doesn't help to discover who you really are. The problem is that seeing through this illusion requires that you realize that the determined person who is doing the searching for the answers is the obstacle standing in the way. If there is great determination to find answers this suggests a strong belief in the person who is looking for answers. But the stronger the belief that *you* are doing the searching—the more difficult it is to see that 'you' who is doing the searching is what has to disappear. Or as Nisargadatta says, 'the seeker and the sought are one.'"

As Dave turned the truck toward the lane, Alex called out, "Start meditating and then come back and talk some more. And do some more work on that wall!"

Dave honked twice as the truck splashed down the lane.

Alex's list of 50 things do-it-yourself investors should consider

Don't be over confident or try to beat the experts.

1. Know the difference between the various service providers in the financial services industry.

Licensed salespeople may know a lot—or almost nothing— about investing, and they have a conflict of interest when making investment recommendations. Many investors would do better by using a robo- advisor or doing it themselves with a portfolio of exchange traded funds (ETFS) than by working with a financial advisor who picks individual stocks. Another choice is investment counselors, who are generally chartered financial analysts (CFA) and often have years of portfolio management experience. They act as fiduciaries, provide useful performance reports and the best ones can add value compared with an ETF portfolio.

2. Consider who you're competing against before you trade individual stocks.

Think of it as a contest. Most of the trading on the stock market is done by professionals. So when the do-it-yourself (DIY) investor buys or sells a stock, someone with more information, smarts and discipline (e.g., a hedge-fund manager) may be on the other side of the trade. If the professional wants to buy what you want to sell, ask yourself what that professional knows that you don't. An individual investor trying to beat the professionals is like a weekend golfer expecting to consistently beat Tiger Woods.

3. Respect the complexity of the stock market.

Some investors believe that if they know everything there is to know about a company they'll be able to predict how the stock price will move. The reality is that unpredictable events such as global conflicts, unexpected innovations, new competitors, government intervention, what happens in China, social trends or an earthquake in Russia can have a significant and unpredictable impact on the price of a stock.

4. Understand that a high IQ is not enough to beat the market.

Realize that the investors on the other side of the trade (investment managers, professional traders and hedge-fund managers) are also very intelligent and they have more information and a disciplined buy/sell strategy. Sir Isaac Newton was pretty intelligent—and he lost everything in 1720.

5. Have someone challenge you on your investment ideas.

When working on your own it's difficult not to fall in love with your own ideas. Individuals working in a group have to champion their ideas and convince others of their merits while other members are doing the same with their ideas. Challenging each other makes it more likely that the group will make a wise decision.

6. Index at least part of your portfolio.

Some mandates (e.g., large-capitalization US stocks) are followed so closely by so many analysts that it's practically impossible for an individual to discover information not already factored into the share price. Investors who want exposure to these investment mandates should follow the example of the large pension funds that get this exposure by buying a low-cost index fund or an EFT.

7. Understand that what you read in the *Wall Street Journal* is old news.

Professional investment managers usually know what's happening in a company long before developments are reported in the newspapers. By the time DIY investors read about it, it's usually too late for a profitable trade. DIY investors should also understand that experts in the media are expressing opinions; it's easy to find other experts with the opposite opinion.

8. Understand that with age you will eventually want some help with investing.

Sooner or later individuals lose confidence in their ability to make wise investment choices. Make the transition to a professional manager while you are still able to complete a critical assessment of the manager's integrity and ability.

Follow a disciplined investment process.

9. Develop standard operating procedures (SOPS).

When firefighters run into a burning building they don't try to formulate a plan of action on the fly. Instead, they follow their SOPS, which they've practiced until their response is automatic. Similarly, when markets are crashing or soaring investors should not have to think about what they're going to do, they should follow their SOPS as written in their Investment Policy Statement (IPS).

10. Develop an Investment Policy Statement.

A written IPS explains the investment process, the acceptable range for different sectors or investment mandates and the benchmarks against which performance will be measured. Rebalancing according to your IPS is a simple but effective investment strategy. A written IPS is like a touchstone that will help you avoid making decisions based on emotions.

11. Simplify your investment portfolio.

DIY investors often hold too many small positions—positions that could double in value and still make no appreciable difference in the portfolio. Though they are too small to be useful, these positions are a distraction. DIY investors may also hold complicated structured securities that make it difficult to understand fees, asset mix or inherent risk. They may have legacy mutual funds and small accounts, which makes it difficult to rebalance or even know how much is in each of the different investment mandates.

12. Don't try to time the market.

Most investment managers agree that no one can consistently predict the top or bottom of the market. Many can pick the top and get out at the best time, but these people rarely get back in at the bottom. In most cases those who move into cash at the right time often delay getting back into the market because when it's at the bottom they expect it will go even lower. Disciplined rebalancing is a better strategy.

13. Trade less frequently.

With a well-designed portfolio and a disciplined process, you might need to make only a few changes each year.

14. Concentrate on establishing the time to sell a stock position rather than on trying to determine when to invest in a new position.

It is easier and more interesting to think about buying than selling, but if you don't have a sell strategy you don't have an investment strategy. There is also less emotional attachment to a stock you've never owned than to one you've owned for years. However, deciding which stock to sell and the price to sell it at is just as important as buying at the right time. Investors should record their reasons for buying, their expectations for the stock and the target selling price—this way, DIY investors will get a better idea of how right or wrong they are in their expectations.

15. Focus more on asset allocation and less on security selection.

The investing process is generally more important than the investment products. Studies confirm that over the longer term, most investors would be happier with their results if they focused more on the allocation among investment mandates and less on security selection (which specific stocks to choose).

16. Realize that you can't delay or avoid making decisions.

Although some wish to avoid making decisions, this is impossible. A decision to do nothing is the same as a decision to move to the existing asset allocation and to buy the existing portfolio of securities at today's market price.

Focus on managing risk.

17. Don't put all your investment eggs in one basket.

Not only does this mean higher risk than necessary, it means you have nothing to rebalance to. When stocks go down you want to be able to sell fixed-income investments to generate the cash to buy more stocks while they're cheap. If you're all in stocks all you can do is hold onto them—you'll have no cash to buy more.

18. Take only as much risk as necessary to achieve your goals.

Your investment portfolio should be goals-based. If you can achieve your goals with a return of 4.5% you should not have an asset mix designed to earn 6.5%, as this would mean taking more risk than is necessary. A financial plan is the best tool to determine the proper asset mix. If you don't have a financial plan that shows the rate of return required to achieve your goals you're probably taking either too much or too little risk.

19. Diversify by sectors.

Many DIY investors are over-concentrated in core sectors of the market and don't hold enough in "enhancement mandates" that can reduce volatility and enhance returns (e.g., small-capitalization stocks, corporate bonds, commercial real estate, emerging markets). Some investors are over-concentrated in a few stocks. Many wealthy people made their money by holding concentrated positions, but they keep their wealth by being well diversified.

20. Diversify internationally.

Canadian investors, for example, should know that almost 70% of the Canadian market is concentrated in only three sectors of the economy: financials, energy and materials. Exposure to international companies can provide good diversification and exposure to sectors and industries such as technology, healthcare, pharmaceuticals, consumer staples, media, chemicals, electronics, automobiles and more.

21. Limit security risk and market risk.

You can't avoid market risk and still have a diversified portfolio, but there's no need to take undue risk on individual stocks (think Nortel or Lehman Brothers) as well as market risk. DIY investors can limit individual security risk by investing in a portfolio of ETFS. The robo-advisor EFF models make a lot of sense.

22. Focus more on managing risk and less on maximizing potential returns.

Investment managers focus on managing risk, whereas most DIY investors focus on the potential for returns. Before DIY investors purchase or sell a security they should assess how the change will affect the risk of the portfolio as a whole.

23. Understand that in a rising market we all think we have a high tolerance for risk.

The problem is that markets always correct—sometimes by as much as 50%. It's only in a falling market that you can properly assess your tolerance for risk. In a falling market investors sometimes discover that their tolerance for risk is lower than they thought, and then their emotions take over and they sell at the wrong time.

24. Be sure to address all the risks.

Returns are easy to measure but it's more difficult to measure risk. Sometimes DIY investors begin to understand risk only after it's too late. Often they pay too little attention to risks such as inflation, currency, interest rates, income tax, liquidity, over-concentration and hidden fees.

25. Understand that a stop-loss order won't always protect you.

The problem with a stop-loss order (a standing order to sell a stock if its price drops below a certain point) is that if the market takes a sudden intra-day plunge of more than 20% it may not be possible to fill the order until the market bottoms. Then the sell order may be filled—just before the market rebounds.

26. Remember the mathematics of a loss and a recovery.

If you have a stock that trades at $100 and it drops by 50% so that it's trading at $50, you need a 100% increase in value just to get back to the break-even point. Over time slow and steady returns (while not as exciting) will deliver a better result than higher returns, which are punctuated by steep losses.

Focus on the big picture: Know your goals, have a plan.

27. Take time to clarify your financial goals.

If you don't know what you want to achieve you'll not know the rate of return you should be aiming for. Maybe you already have enough and you should be enjoying your wealth, or maybe you need to change your investment strategy and level of spending to achieve the things that matter most to you. Money is of no value unless you can use it to achieve goals and increase happiness.

28. Address important estate issues.

The reality is that we can't take it with us. As they say, the Brink's truck doesn't follow the hearse. If it's almost certain that you will have a surplus when you pass away, manage your affairs to get enjoyment by giving it away while you're living rather than having it dispersed after you're gone.

29. If you have a spouse, keep him or her involved.

Even if you choose to continue as a DIY investor it may be helpful to develop a relationship with an investment manager so that your spouse will know where to turn for help if needed. If you don't establish such a relationship while the more knowledgeable spouse is still around to provide advice, the surviving spouse may be the victim of the first salesperson who appears on the scene.

30. Understand the danger when more than money is at stake.

If a DIY investor is close to retirement or is retired and is financially secure, a big investing mistake could mean more than frustration and the children receiving a smaller inheritance. It might mean living a reduced lifestyle. When financial security and retirement lifestyle are at stake, it's even more important to manage risk.

31. Focus on the right time horizon.

Most investors save for long-term goals such as retirement. For this objective, it's the value of the portfolio at the date of retirement that's important. Short-term drops in value are not a concern and in fact, when you are following a disciplined investment process, a drop in value can be an opportunity to rebalance. It makes no sense to avoid volatility over the next 30 years (before you need the money) if a more volatile portfolio will give you more money when you do need it.

32. Have a financial plan that shows how things will work out under different assumptions.

A properly prepared financial plan provides financial peace of mind by showing how things will work out in different situations. It also shows the rate of return necessary to achieve your goals and what level of risk and what asset mix are most appropriate to earn that rate.

33. Understand the difference between investment income and cash flow.

Investment income consists of interest, dividends and capital gains. To maintain your lifestyle in retirement you need cash flow from your investments. One tax-efficient way to get the needed cash flow is to realize some of your capital gains. Some investors overlook the potential cash flow from capital gains and feel that to get the cash flow they require they should invest almost exclusively in securities that generate interest and dividends.

Avoid emotional responses.

34. Keep your emotions out of the way.

Don't hang onto losers to avoid recognizing your mistakes. Remain emotionally detached from security positions. Don't hold stocks you would not buy today at today's price, hoping they will recover. Hope is not a strategy. Don't take extreme views, thinking a terrible collapse is imminent or that good times are here to stay and we'll never see another 50% market crash.

35. Treat all your money the same, even if it's in different pools.

Money is money and whether you accumulated it through a disciplined savings program, an inheritance, a bonus or a windfall profit, all of your capital should be managed with the same level of care.

36. Don't overreact to either good news or bad.

Sometimes a company may release unexpected bad news and its share price drops within minutes, or an unexpected good thing happens and the price pops up suddenly. Usually within a year the impact of this event is negligible, leaving DIY investors to regret selling when the price was down or buying when the price spiked higher.

37. Don't expect a current trend to continue.

It is human nature to expect the current trend to continue. In a bull (rising) market we expect stock prices to continue to go higher. In a bear (falling) market we expect prices to continue to drop. The reality is that trends always reverse themselves. As a general rule investors should sell into a market that has risen significantly and buy into a market that has dropped significantly. The way to do this without trying to time the market is to rebalance your portfolio in a disciplined manner whenever it gets out of whack.

Measure performance.

38. Keep score: Track your performance against the proper composite benchmark.

Don't kid yourself about how well you're doing. One simple solution is comparing your actual performance against a benchmark robo-advisor portfolio of exchange traded funds. Don't be like those golfers who really enjoy the game and think they play better than average, but don't keep score and only remember their good shots, forgetting all the four-putts. Most DIY investors are satisfied when they make a positive return but rarely do they compare that return with the proper composite benchmark.

39. Calculate the cost of underperformance.

Based on experience, I estimate that DIY investors who do not measure performance against the proper benchmark are underperforming by over 2% per annum. On a $500,000 portfolio, underperforming by 2% per annum over the next 25 years could mean spending $400,000 less in retirement. That's more than enough to buy a house!

Pay attention to income tax and investment fees.

40. Keep income tax efficiency in mind.

Income tax is our biggest expense. It's your after-tax rate of return that's important. Tax efficiency can be achieved at the security level, the individual manager level or the macro level by choosing the proper location for different managers and securities, by choosing dividends or capital gains over interest income, by income splitting, through estate planning, through tax-exempt insurance or with a corporate class share structure.

41. BUT—don't let the "tax tail" wag the dog.

Don't allow your portfolio to become over-concentrated, exposing you to more risk than necessary because you want to delay paying capital gains tax. All things being equal it's wise to delay the payment of tax, but it's a mistake when the delay requires you to be poorly diversified or to hold on to a security you should sell.

42. Be sure to harvest your capital losses.

Capital losses should be recognized and used to reduce the tax otherwise payable on capital gains.

43. Be sure you understand all the fees you're paying.

Fees are one of the biggest obstacles for investors who want to at least match the appropriate benchmark. It's not always obvious what the fees are on mutual funds and structured products, so take the time to ensure you understand all the embedded fees and trading costs. If some of your money is managed by a financial advisor ask for a written explanation of all fees.

44. Make sure you're getting value for the fees you pay.

In many cases DIY investors start doing their own investing because they feel they are paying too much in fees. Any fee is too much if you receive no value for it, but higher fees may be justified if significant value is added. The focus should not be on fees per se but on value. And to be able to measure the value added you need reports that show performance (net of fees) compared with the proper composite benchmarks.

Don't act on bad information.

45. Understand that some professional managers do consistently beat the market.

Few mutual funds consistently beat the market, but that is largely because of fees, over-diversification and "closet indexing." Just as some professional athletes are better than others (and get paid more), some investment managers in each investment mandate have built 10-year records of adding significant value.

46. Don't act on tips from friends or colleagues.

Tips are like rumors; they're usually based on faulty information. If the tip does result in a profit it may have been based on insider information, in which case anyone who acts on the information could have a legal problem.

47. Understand reversion to the mean.

Reversion to the mean is a mathematical concept that means that if either an individual stock or the market as a whole is currently trading above the long-term average, it will eventually trade below the long-term average—and vice versa.

48. Don't fall for the "it's only a paper loss" line.

Investors sometimes fool themselves by saying a loss is not a loss until they sell the affected holdings. That's like saying you can avoid gaining weight if you avoid stepping on the scales. If you bought a stock at $10 and it now trades at $2, you have lost money. Failing to recognize this fact simply delays realizing the tax loss.

49. Understand that "buy and hold" is a not a sound long-term investment strategy.

DYI investors who like to buy and hold should realize that this strategy works well in a bull market but not so well in a secular bear market. This idea became popular after the bear market that ended in 1982. In the 70s anyone who followed a buy-and-hold strategy would have suffered greatly. In 1988 Japan's Nikkei Index was at about 40,000; today it's at about 16,000. You wouldn't want to be a Japanese buy-and-hold investor.

50. Understand that a particular investing style (e.g., value investing or growth investing) will not always be the best style.

The investment style that is most effective will change from time to time. Some years, value investing is best and sometimes growth investing is best. Few investment managers are expert at both styles. If professional managers don't expect to be able switch from one style to another and consistently beat the market, the odds of a part-time DIY investor successfully switching from one style to another are low.

Summary: How to manage your money wisely

- Don't be over confident or try to beat the experts.

- Follow a disciplined investment process.

- Focus on managing risk.

- Focus on the big picture: Know your goals, have a plan.

- Avoid emotional responses.

- Measure performance.

- Pay attention to income tax and investment fees.

- Don't act on bad information.

Alex's list of 21 ways to reduceinvestment management fees

It's never made more sense than it does now to control investment management fees. Years ago, when investors expected a balanced portfolio to deliver an average return of 10%, a 2% fee might have been okay. But when expected returns are closer to 4% you have to realize that although you're taking 100% of the risk, a 2% fee would eat up half your total return.

All other things being equal, a higher fee means a lower return. We should remember, however, that the main objective is not to minimize fees. The main objective is to achieve your goals. If a reasonable fee increases the odds of achieving your goals, that fee is justified. If you're not receiving value, even a tiny fee is too much.

Investors want value for the fees they pay. And one way to measure value is by comparing actual results with those of the appropriate benchmark or to the return generated by a robo-advisor portfolio with the same level of risk.

1. Ask for a discount.

Many financial advisors will offer a discount if you ask. No advisor will offer a discount if you seem happy with the higher fee. The best time to ask for a discount is when you are starting a new advisor relationship, before you sign the application form. If you've been with the same advisor for 10 or 15 years, be aware that fees are generally lower now than they were when you signed on as a client. If new clients are paying a lower fee, you should as well!

2. Buy and hold.

This strategy triggers the lowest fees and also defers the payment of capital gains tax. One disadvantage of a buy-and-hold approach is that you don't get to lock in profits by rebalancing. Without rebalancing, your portfolio may eventually become higher risk because the allocation to equities usually grows faster than the allocation to fixed income.

3. Use exchange traded funds (ETF).

Index-tracking ETFS have lower fees than mutual funds and your return will be close to the return of the market. A portfolio of ETFS will likely give you a better return than a portfolio of stocks that you pick on your own or that your advisor recommends.

4. Do it yourself.

Most DIY investors should use ETFS rather than individual stocks. DIY investors can be blind to their own shortcomings so make sure you measure your performance against a robo-advisor portfolio with the same level of risk. If your performance doesn't at least match that of an appropriate benchmark, reconsider doing your own investing.

5. Use robo-advisors.

Robo-advisors are financial advice companies that provide online portfolio management services with minimal human intervention. Most robo-advisors employ algorithms such as modern portfolio theory to construct efficient ETF portfolios. Fees are a bit higher than a DIY investor using ETFS, but the disciplined rebalancing should more than offset the slightly higher fees. A big plus is that robo-advisors are licensed as portfolio managers and are therefore required to adhere to the fiduciary standard, which gives investors more protection than the "suitability" standard most financial advisors adhere to.

6. Use a Private Investment Counsel (PIC) firm.

PIC firms are the true professionals in the financial services industry and they offer active rather than passive investment management. PIC firms have lower fees than either mutual funds or full-service bank advisors, they follow a disciplined investment process and they offer better performance reporting. They also adhere to the fiduciary standard.

7. Pay commissions rather than fees.

A well-managed account requires few transactions, so paying normal commissions per trade will usually mean lower overall costs than paying an annual fee based on the size of the account. And it makes no sense to pay a management fee on cash or on securities you never intend to sell.

8. Ask for a written description of all fees.

When it's going to be put in writing, advisors are more careful about estimating fees (and more likely to mention the embedded fees you pay indirectly).

9. Avoid structured products.

The highest fees and costs (largely hidden) are found in structured products that usually have some sort of guarantee that you'll get your capital back. But it's a mistake to pay a high fee for a product that will reduce volatility during the period when you don't need the money, if by accepting some volatility you'll have more money when you do need it. You should be comfortable with the volatility associated with the asset mix necessary to get the rate of return needed to achieve your goals. If you're not comfortable with this level of volatility it's better to reduce spending than to pay the high fees associated with structured products.

10. Avoid performance fees.

Performance fees are usually found in hedge funds and you need to ensure that the "hurdle rate" and the "high-water mark" make sense. The hurdle rate is the rate of return above which the performance fee is triggered and the high-water mark ensures that you don't pay a performance fee when the return only allows you to recover from a previous loss. Be aware that a performance fee creates an incentive for the investment manager to take more risk with your money.

11. Trade less frequently.

Frequent trading is usually a sign that the investor is acting emotionally rather than following a disciplined investment process. It would be unusual for market conditions to dictate rebalancing more than once per year. Someone once said that an investment portfolio is like a bar of soap—the more it's handled the smaller it becomes.

12. Consolidate your accounts with one advisor.

Usually the more assets an advisor is managing the lower the fee will be. But you should consolidate only if the advisor follows a disciplined investment process, creates a goals-based asset allocation, provides an Investment Policy Statement that shows benchmarks and is sufficiently detailed to hold the advisor accountable, provides reports that compare performance with benchmarks, and uses best-in-class rather than in-house managers.

13. Know your trading expense ratio (TER).

The TER is in addition to the management expense ratio (MER). The TER typically adds between 0.01% and 1% to the annual cost (the average is about 0.15%). TER comparisons are most useful when comparing similar types of investment mandates.

14. Avoid balanced funds.

The MER for one popular balanced fund (70% equities and 30% fixed income) is 10% higher than what you would pay if you bought the same equity fund and the same bond fund individually from the same mutual fund company in the same proportions. While the MER will be higher with the balanced fund this may be justified since the benefit of rebalancing may offset the higher cost.

15. Avoid deferred sales charge (DSC) mutual funds.

Typically, the sales charge on these funds is 6% and declines to 0% in five to seven years. Unfortunately, many investors trigger the DSC fee because they grow impatient when the fund under-performs compared with its peer group. In other cases investors feel locked in and are reluctant to move out of a DSC fund even if the manager consistently underperforms his or her peers.

16. Avoid initial public offerings (IPOS).

Investors often buy IPOS because it appears they can make the purchase while paying no commission. The reality is that most

IPOS fall in value within one year. So investors can often do better by skipping the IPO and buying the stock at a lower price in about a year's time.

17. Avoid segregated mutual funds.

Segregated mutual funds are a type of high-fee fund (the MER is usually over 3%) that offer benefits such as guarantees at death or maturity, creditor protection, avoidance of probate and the ability to lock in profits with "resets." Typically, investors have to hold the funds for 15 years to get a 100% guarantee. It would be unlikely that over a 15-year period a well-balanced investment would not grow, so a guarantee that gives you back only your capital in 15 years is of questionable value.

18. Understand bond commissions.

Investors should be aware that the commissions on bond purchases (including strip bonds) are usually calculated on the higher maturity value of the bond—not on the purchase price. Retail investors can usually save money on the fees and the spread by buying bond ETFS.

19. Consolidate to get premium pricing.

Some fund companies will reduce the MER by 10 to 30 basis points if a family unit has more than $100,000 invested in mutual funds of a single fund company. Some fund companies have expanded the definition of "household" to encourage this type of consolidation.

20. Make the investment management fee tax deductible.

The MER for a mutual fund or ETF is paid by the fund itself and is therefore not immediately deductible for the investor. Fees charged by investment counseling firms, however, are billed and paid directly by the investor and therefore may be income tax deductible.

21. Change advisors.

Investment management fees have fallen. Most advisors opening up new accounts today charge less than they did to open the same size account 10 years ago. If you have been with the same advisor for over 15 years and the fee has not changed, it may be possible to get a lower fee just by shopping around.

Oscar Wilde said a cynic is a person "who knows the cost of everything and the value of nothing." Wise investors pay attention to fees but their primary focus is on determining whether they receive value for the fees they pay.

Fees are important, but the after-fee performance is even more important. Unfortunately, few investors receive a performance report that shows how they're doing compared with the appropriate benchmark. If investors don't know whether they are on track to achieve their goals or how they are performing, they can't know whether they're receiving value for the fees they pay. In my experience most investors who are not measuring performance against a proper benchmark are underperforming that benchmark by about 2% per annum. If a 2% higher return would make a difference to you, you really should measure your performance.

Alex's article on the value of Investment Policy Statements

Over the long term, both excellent and very poor investment results can often be explained by the presence or absence of an Investment Policy Statement (IPS). If you don't have one—or don't know what it is—read on. If you think it makes sense to have a blueprint before you start building a house or a recipe before you start baking, you'll understand why it makes sense to have an IPS to guide you in the investment process.

Investors should understand that the investment *process* is the most important thing—more important in the long run than the investment products. The IPS will set out the objectives, the investment strategy and other relevant information for the management of the portfolio. The IPS provides guidance and protection for everyone involved.

Emotional reactions (such as fear and greed) can be a significant problem for most investors; the IPS helps take emotion out of the equation. It enables you to decide in a logical way on the appropriateness of investments, the investment strategy or the investment managers. The IPS helps you manage your response to both bad news and exceedingly optimistic market forecasts. If you work with investment managers it becomes their guideline, and any disputes can be resolved by determining whether the manager followed the guidelines. With an IPS there is less likelihood of a dispute because the responsibilities of each party are clearly stated.

A properly prepared IPS will help you to

- Focus on the investing process rather than investment products
- Better manage your portfolio while spending only a couple of hours each quarter
- Choose the proper long-term/neutral asset allocation
- Set out the acceptable high and low ranges for each asset class
- Manage your response to rising and falling markets
- Avoid paralysis and indecision
- Understand the risks, including downside risk (negative performance results), and take no more risk than necessary
- Identify the proper benchmark so you can measure and monitor performance
- Ensure that your expectations are realistic
- Feel confident and secure about your investment strategy
- Consider investment constraints, such as not investing in alcohol or tobacco companies if you so choose, or not holding derivative security products
- Make rebalancing and tactical changes with confidence
- Ensure that liquidity needs are met without holding more cash than necessary
- Make logical decisions when changing investment managers or buying or selling securities

- Ensure that you address tax efficiency

- Control investment costs

- Ensure that each party understands his or her responsibilities

- Minimize the possibility of disputes or litigation

- Get you involved in the investment process—your oversight is important

If an IPS is so important why doesn't everyone have one? The reality is that any tool that helps generate better results for investors has the opposite impact on the profits of banks and mutual fund companies. When you are emotional, jumping in and out of investments, and when you pay high fees, the banks and mutual fund companies make more money. These firms therefore have no incentive to promote the use of a properly prepared IPS.

From the investment firm's point of view, the problem with an IPS is that it

- Forces advisors to focus on the investment process rather than on selling investment products

- Requires full disclosure of all fees

- Sets out the benchmark that makes advisors accountable

- Removes the mystery and makes investing seem simple

- Requires time to prepare and to review periodically

The industry gets around the lack of an IPS by using the Know Your Client (KYC) form. This form is a poor substitute for a properly prepared IPS; some would say the KYC form is designed primarily to protect the brokerage firm or banking institution from lawsuits: if a client suffers greater-than-necessary losses from being in the wrong asset mix or by investing in speculative securities, the institution can point to the KYC form and say, "but you said you were comfortable with high risk."

There are two problems with the KYC form. First, your answers to its questions are unreliable because when you opened the account and filled in the form you were likely calm and rational and didn't know how you would react when you started to panic. Fear is an emotional response, not a logical one. Second, even if you do have nerves of steel, why take more risk than necessary to achieve your goals?

It's easy to create an IPS if you want one—many examples are available on the Internet. The more difficult task is asking your advisor or salesperson for a proper IPS.

An IPS is most likely to be used by institutional investors (such as foundations and pension plans), wealthy investors who use a family office and clients who deal with investment counselors. In these cases an IPS exists because the parties involved are knowledgeable and experienced. Investment managers who want to work with wealthy, sophisticated investors know they need to demonstrate their professionalism or they'll not win the account so they prepare a proper IPS.

An IPS is least likely to be used by investors who deal with a mutual fund salesperson; by full-service brokers, wealth managers and financial planners; by clients of bank-owned brokerage firms; and by DYI investors. In these cases the advisor usually has less professional training and the clients are less sophisticated and may not be aware of the importance of an IPS. If an IPS is not expected it will probably not be offered. DYI investors also need an IPS. In this case it is not to control fees or set the criteria for manager selection but to enable you to control your emotions and to make it easier to follow a disciplined approach.

Review your IPS annually. If your goals or risk tolerance

have changed, you may need to change your IPS. But there's no need to change it as a result of changing market conditions or a different market outlook. In fact, the IPS anticipates market volatility and provides guidelines for what investment changes are appropriate when the markets go through their regular bull and bear cycles.

The following are some of the sections you can expect to find in a well-prepared IPS:

Scope and Purpose
All sections of the IPS are briefly discussed to provide a clear picture of what it's all about.

Governance
Responsibilities of the advisor, portfolio manager, custodian and investor are clearly explained. This will help resolve any disputes that arise.

Return Objectives
Based on the client's objectives, the required rate of return is stated. This helps in deciding on the asset allocation for the portfolio and the associated downside risk.

Risk Tolerance
The client's ability and willingness to take risks are decided subjectively.

Asset Allocation
Based on the required rate of return, the asset allocation and the allowable ranges for asset classes are clearly defined. Asset allocation is how much exposure the portfolio should have to particular asset classes. These guidelines create a basis for dispute resolution if a problem arises.

Rebalancing Strategy
A clearly defined rebalancing strategy necessitates regular portfolio monitoring and action at appropriate times without succumbing to an emotional response to market fluctuations.

Performance Benchmarks
The predetermined performance benchmark enables evaluation of the manager's performance. Performance versus the benchmark also shows a DIY investor whether you should fire yourself and hire a professional manager.

Investment Manager Selection
Clearly laying out the criteria for manager selection allows an investor to engage only those managers who meet the criteria.

Portfolio Constraints
Liquidity requirements for the next year provide an idea of how much money should be kept as cash and cash equivalents. Time horizon is an important factor in deciding the asset allocation. The strategy to minimize income tax is also clearly stated. Consider legal constraints if there are any special conditions for trust assets, etc. Unique circumstances, such as socially responsible investing, restrictions on tobacco or alcohol companies, and the policy on using leverage, options, futures, etc., should be clearly stated here.

Investment Strategies
Clearly defining investment strategies, such as rebalancing strategies and when to make tactical shifts, will help keep emotions in check during turbulent market conditions.

Watch List Criteria
Clearly stated manager performance objectives help determine when a manager should be placed on the watch list.

Fees

Fees are a significant drag on portfolio performance. Fee structures for all parties involved should be transparent and aligned with the client's interests.

Review

The IPS requires periodic review; the frequency of the reviews should be stated in the document.

IPS Agreement

Having all parties involved in the investment management process sign an agreement makes them aware of their responsibilities and helps in dispute resolution should the need arise.

In summary, the main benefits of an IPS are as follows:

- It forces you to focus on the investment process rather than investment products.

- It helps you manage your response to volatile stock markets.

- It enables you to measure performance against a benchmark.

- It explains fees, the rebalancing strategy and the potential downside risk and it reduces the probability of disputes.

- It helps ensure that you are taking no more risk than necessary to achieve your financial goals.

- It enables you to hold your financial advisors accountable.

Further Reading

Wealth management

Clason, George S. *The Richest Man in Babylon*. Penguin, 1926. 19th edition, Createspace, 2014.

Deans, Thomas William. *Every Family's Business: 12 Common Sense Questions to Protect Your Wealth*, 2nd edition. Détente Financial Press, 2009.

Deans, Thomas William. *Willing Wisdom: 7 Questions Successful Families Ask*. Détente Financial Press, 2013.

Skidelsky, Robert, and Edward Skidelsky. *How Much Is Enough?: Money and the Good Life*. Allen Lane, 2012.

Zen practice

Beck, Charlotte Joko. *Everyday Zen: Love & Work*. Edited by Steve Smith. Harper, 1989.

Beck, Charlotte Joko. *Nothing Special: Living Zen*. With Steve Smith. HarperCollins, 1993.

Herrigel, Eugen. *Zen in the Art of Archery*. Pantheon, 1948. Vintage Books, 1989.

Hesse, Hermann. *Siddhartha*. 1922. Bantam, 1951.

Hood, Bruce. *The Self Illusion: How the Social Brain Creates Identity*. Oxford University Press, 2012.

Nisargadatta Maharaj, Sri. I *Am That: Talks with Sri Nisargadatta Maharaj*. Revised and edited by Sudhakar S. Dikshit. Acorn, 1973.

Nisargadatta Maharaj, Sri. *The Experience of Nothingness: Sri Nisargadatta Maharaj's Talks on Realizing the Infinite*. Edited by Robert Powell. Blue Dove, 1996.

Oriah, Mountain Dreamer. *The Invitation*. HarperCollins 2006.

Young, Shinzen. *The Science of Enlightenment – How Meditation Works*. Sounds True, Boulder, Colorado, 2016.

About the author

Warren MacKenzie studied religion, philosophy and psychology at university, and after completing an education degree at Dalhousie University he began teaching school in Nova Scotia. He left teaching to become a Chartered Professional Accountant. Eventually he left public accounting to work as a financial advisor with a major brokerage firm, where he earned the Certified Financial Planner and Certified Investment Management Analyst designations. He is the author of *The Unbiased Advisor* and co-author of *New Rules of Retirement* and *The C.A.R.P. Financial Planning Guide*. He has written numerous investment articles for magazines and is a regular contributor to the Financial Facelift column in *The Globe and Mail*.

Warren's meditation experience started in the 1970s and his beliefs have been greatly influenced by Sri Nisargadatta Maharaj, author of *I Am That*, and Charlotte Joko Beck, who taught at the Zen Center of San Diego.

After years of and study and meditation Warren found the answers he was looking for and what he learned from this study helps him enjoy life to the fullest. He is married, with three children and ten grandchildren, and currently works with a Private Investment Counsel firm. On summer weekends he can often be found adding rocks to his drystone wall.